ALSO BY THE HARVARD LAMPOON

Nightlight
Bored of the Rings

THE HARVARD LAMPOON

A TOUCHSTONE BOOK
Published by Simon & Schuster
New York   London   Toronto   Sydney   New Delhi

THE HUNGER PAINS

A PARODY

Touchstone
A Division of Simon & Schuster, Inc.
1230 Avenue of the Americas
New York, NY 10020

First Touchstone trade paperback edition February 2012

TOUCHSTONE and colophon are registered
trademarks of Simon & Schuster, Inc.

For information about special discounts for bulk purchases,
please contact Simon & Schuster Special Sales at
1-866-506-1949 or business@simonandschuster.com.

The Simon & Schuster Speakers Bureau can bring authors to your
live event. For more information or to book an event contact the
Simon & Schuster Speakers Bureau at 1-866-248-3049 or visit our
website at www.simonspeakers.com.

Edited by Charles A. Sull, Jonathan D. Adler, and Allison L. Averill

Designed by Joy O'Meara

Manufactured in the United States of America

5 7 9 10 8 6

Library of Congress Cataloging-in-Publication Data
Harvard Lampoon (Organization)
The hunger pains : a parody / The Harvard Lampoon.
       p. cm.
   1. Collins, Suzanne. 2. Hunger Games—
      Parodies, imitations, etc. I. Title.
          PS3600.A6 H33 2012
813'.6   2011040718

ISBN 978-1-4516-6820-9
ISBN 978-1-4516-6821-6 (ebook)

To Joseph F. Hickey

1

I awake to the sound of a growling stomach. It's not mine. It's the cat's. "Shut up, Butterball," I moan, as I push him off the bed. He hits the ground with a thud. "Bark!" goes the cat. I try to go back to sleep but it's no use. Today is Super Fun Day.

I tiptoe across the dirt floor to the other side of the room to avoid waking my mother. Butterball has recovered from crashing into the floor and licks my leg annoyingly. He's hungry.

I look in the cabinet for some food. The cabinet is where we keep our small food supply. It's also where my little sister sleeps. Her name is Prin, which is short for Princess. Butterball is Prin's cat. When I open the cabinet, Prin is snuggled up against an empty box of cookies. She looks so cute.

The only thing I see for Butterball to eat is a small pile of moldy carrots. I carefully reach my hand into the cabinet and grab them. Prin stirs for a moment but doesn't wake up. *"Phew!"* I say, really loudly. Now she wakes up.

"Close the cabinet, you idiot!" she shouts.

"I'm sorry," I say. I lean in to give her a peck on the cheek, but she slams the cabinet door in my face.

I toss the carrots down to Butterball. He looks up at me and growls. You see, Butterball and I are not exactly the closest of friends. I remember when Prin first brought him home. He was the biggest, ugliest cat I had ever seen, weighing probably fifty pounds, with a wet, black nose and floppy ears and a tongue that just wouldn't stay in his mouth but insisted on slurp, slurp, slurping all over the place. His thick golden fur was full of fleas, and every time I threw a rubber newspaper out the window, the dumb old cat would run to retrieve it and bring it back, panting. He was repulsive.

"No way, Prin," I said at the time, "you can't keep him." Then I led Butterball outside to drown him in the puddle at the end of our driveway, but the puddle was so shallow that his long snout wouldn't fit under the water. "Fine," I relented, "you can keep the stupid cat."

So we kept Butterball. Not many people have pets where I'm from. I live in District 12, one of twelve districts that make up Peaceland. District 12 is the poorest district. While some affectionately call it "the Dirty Dozen," most call it "a Terrible Place to Live." My neighborhood, the worst in District 12, is known as the Crack.

I look down at Butterball as he chows down on those delicious rotting carrots. I should have saved a few for myself. For a moment, I envy Butterball. Today is just another ordinary day for that dumb cat. He'll chase his tail and catch

Frisbees in the park without a care in the world. But for me, today is different. It's Super Fun Day.

The sun is rising. It's time to hunt. I pull my boots out from under the bed, the pair my father gave me before he died. Once they're on, I'm ready to go. I'm careful not to let the door slam on my way out. Once it closes softly, I open up the mail slot and yell back into the house, "I'm going hunting!" I set off to meet my hunting partner, Carol Handsomestein.

The streets of District 12 are eerily empty today. The regular clatter of keyboards and ringing of telephones that usually fills the air has fallen silent as the anxious pall brought by the arrival of Super Fun Day descends over the town like a pillow and duct tape over the face of an unwanted pet.

A man raises the District 12 flag outside his house as I walk by. It's black, like all the flags in merry old Peaceland. In the center, there's a golden telephone. Each district specializes in one industry, and District 12 is the telemarketing district. Along with the other districts, District 12 once rose up in rebellion against the Capital, which is where all the rich and powerful people of Peaceland live. That didn't go too well. In fact, it went horribly. How horribly? Well, there used to be two hundred districts. Lesson learned.

In order to ensure nobody ever forgets that the rebellion failed and the Capital won and they are in charge and blah, blah, blah, each year they make all twelve districts participate in what is called the Hunger Games. Every district selects two kids, one boy and one girl, to represent them in a big competition. These two kids are called *tributes*, which is short for *tributary*, which is a stream or river that flows into a main stem (or parent) river or a lake.

The Hunger Games aren't exactly fun. If I'm being totally honest, I'd say they suck. Since there are twelve districts, and two tributes from each one, you know there are at least . . . twenty tributes in total. All of them are thrown into an arena somewhere in the wilderness where they have to kill one another until there's only one tribute left. And it's all televised. Most people TiVo it so they can fast forward to the killing.

Now, when they first started, the Hunger Games weren't so bad. The Capital gathered all the tributes and televised them doing some pretty fun stuff: softball tournament, relay race, obstacle course, and jumping rope. The main event was a huge hot dog–eating contest. Everybody would try to get extra hungry before it began, hence the name *Hunger Games*.

But after a few years, the tributes got so competitive with one another that the Games turned violent. A punch in the face here, a kick in the crotch there—soon, the tributes were at one another's throats. And rather than putting a stop to this madness, the Capital encouraged it. After all, it made for great television. So they changed the rules. Instead of fun field games and competitive eating, the Hunger Games became a fight to the death. They still allow softball, but nobody's ever in the mood anymore.

Super Fun Day is the day every year when each district selects its tributes. Everybody gathers in the public square. At a certain time, all the kids in District 12 play the nose game. The two kids who are last to touch their fingers to their noses become tributes. This is also televised, and most people TiVo it as well. It airs at the same time as *Seinfeld* reruns.

That's why the streets are so quiet today. Everybody in all of Peaceland has the day off from work for Super Fun Day. Attendance is mandatory. Anyone who doesn't show up for the announcement risks getting the crap beaten out of them by the Pacemakers, the bunch of elderly Capital thugs who are in charge of each district but are otherwise pretty nice people.

I think about all this as I walk toward the woods to meet Carol. I'm getting close to where we usually meet. Suddenly, I hear a twig snap from a few feet away.

"Think fast!" a voice yells. My head turns just as an arrow whizzes past my face and lodges in the tree next to my head. It's Carol.

"No, you think fast!" I say, and stab him in the leg. He pulls out the knife and we laugh so much.

"Nice one, Catpiss," he says. That's not my real name. My name is actually Kantkiss. Kantkiss Neverclean. Carol calls me Catpiss because the first time we met, I whispered my name so softly that he misheard me. And I had just slipped in a puddle of cat urine. Ever since, Carol likes to tease me by calling me Catpiss. Unfortunately, I can't think of any way to make fun of his name.

Carol and I have known each other for years. He's an excellent hunter and he's incredibly good-looking. Even when he's pulling the guts out of a squirrel, he looks so dreamy. I always let him take the first bite of squirrel heart.

Together, we hunt for food to feed our families and to trade for supplies in District 12. There is a flourishing black market in District 12, known as the Nob. At the Nob, Carol and I often trade with an old woman named Slimey Sue. She's famous for her soups and for having a full mustache and no teeth.

I hunt for my family because my father can no longer provide for us. Don't worry, it's not because he's lazy or anything—it's because he's dead. There was an explosion at the telemarketing office where he worked. He had time to call home just one last time, but his body was incinerated before he could finish the sales pitch. He was halfway through the jingle—"Averill's pudding/Tastes real good/Buy Averill's pudding/Today"—but then he was blown to smithereens. I wanted to tell him how much I was going to miss him, that I promised take care of Prin and my mother forever, but he wouldn't stop singing. He was a true telemarketer.

"All right, let's hunt," Carol says, jolting me back to the present. Carol runs his fingers through his hair, and for a moment, I forget that I live in poverty under an authoritarian government and instead feel like I'm the luckiest girl alive.

We reach the electric fence that separates District 12 from the woods. Because of rolling power outages, it's really only electrified for three or four hours each day, so it's usually safe to climb over. For this reason, I am grateful for the power outages. They're the worst for playing video games, though.

We're not supposed to leave District 12, and doing so carries a severe penalty. Not that they really need to deter people from leaving, considering all the deadly crap out beyond the fence. Mamajams, wagalaks, and even some tuto birds all roam free. But there's also food if you know how to find it. Carol and I don't let fear keep us inside the fence, where we'd otherwise waste away to skin and bones in complete and perfect safety. "District Twelve. Where the safety is good, but other things are less good," I say. One of my many clever maxims.

I step toward the fence. I try to hop over, but my leg gets caught in one of the planks. Dropping down on my belly, I try to shimmy my way under the fence, but I just can't suck in my tummy to get low enough. I'm stuck there wriggling between the fence and the ground when Carol grabs my feet and pulls me out. *He's so strong*, I think to myself. Next I try running straight through the fence, but that doesn't work either. By now I'm pretty dizzy. Finally, I spot a small gate about four feet to my left. I unlatch the gate, push it open, and walk through to the other side. Carol takes a few steps back and then proceeds to hurdle over the fence. *Breathtaking.*

We walk along the fence for about half a mile, ready to hunt. Up ahead, we can see a barn. Carol whispers to me. "I'll go high and you go low." I nod back in agreement. I quietly crouch down and start crawling. Carol walks upright beside me. We're prepared for anything.

We arrive at the barn. Locked in a small wooden pen, a handful of cows are grazing on the grass. The cows that aren't

grazing are eating slop out of a big wheelbarrow beside a napping farmer. *Worthy adversaries.* My heart is racing. *This is so
dangerous!*

I load my bow and send an arrow flying. One of the cows
falls to the ground. We sprint toward it. Carol and I hog-tie
its legs and drag it back to the woods and back through the
electric fence. Back to civilization. Even the cow breathes a
sigh of relief before Carol slits its throat.

I reach inside the cow and grab the meat. I hand Carol
the T-bone and the filet and keep the New York strip and por-
terhouse for myself. It was a great hunt. My shrewdness and
courage will keep us alive for at least a few more days.

That is, *if* my mother decides to actually cook for us. You
see, my mother is a horrible person. After my father died,
she became really bummed out for some reason. She would
hardly ever come out of her room. Prin and I would go for
days without so much as a single bagel bite. That's when I
knew I would have to provide for the family. I quickly learned
to identify the edible berries in the supermarket, to iron
blouses, and to make peanut butter and jelly sandwiches. It's
because of me the three of us are still alive.

Super Fun Day is actually the only day of the year that
my mother looks forward to. She's a huge Hunger Games
fan. She can't get enough of them. So when they arrive each
year, she gets very excited. She goes knocking door-to-door to
make sure every person in District 12 attends the selection
ceremony. She even has a special hat—a Super Fun Day
hat—that she wears for the month leading up to Super Fun
Day in anticipation.

I walk in the door to our house carrying the meat in my arms. Prin is up and dressed, sitting on the floor with Butterball. "Here, Prin," I say, "I got you some lunch for Super Fun Day. Don't eat the meat raw. I'll have to cook it first." With little sisters you can never be too careful.

"I can make my own lunch, Kantkiss. I'm not a moron," she says sweetly.

"I love you, Prin," I say.

"Just shut up."

Prin and I are very close. Most of the time it's the thought of her starving to death that keeps me going day in and day out. I promised my father I would never let anything bad happen to her, and I'll keep that promise. He also made me promise I'd never let anything bad happen to *him*, but I guess I sort of dropped the ball on that one.

I toss the meat into the sink and change into the clothes my mother laid out for me. I tell Prin I'll see her at the selection ceremony, then I set off to get a good seat.

On the way, I run into a girl I know from school. Her name is Badge Underwear. Her father is Mayor Underwear, the mayor of District 12. Neither of us has any real friends, so we're usually forced to pair up for things like the three-legged race and partners yoga.

Badge is wearing a pretty little sundress, not like the ugly tube top my mom picked out for me. But it's easy to wear pretty clothes when you don't have to risk your life hunting every day, like I do.

She's wearing a magnificent golden pin on her dress. Its flash catches my eye. It has a golden ring that encircles an emblem that reads THE CAPITAL SUCKS! I stare at the pin and wonder if it means something.

"Hi, Kantkiss!" she says. "I just want to say good luck at Super Fun Day. I hope neither of us gets picked."

"I hope you get picked!" I reply. I can't stand Badge. She's so stuck-up.

"Very funny," she laughs, walking away.

Soon, I arrive at the public square. The only times people ever come here are for Super Fun Day or to go to the post office. Despite its oppressive rule and a tendency to murder its citizens, I've got to admit that the Capital runs a great post office. I've never had to wait in line for more than a couple of minutes, and the censors are very polite when they read your mail.

In the square, all the children of District 12 begin to take their places for the nose game. Many are practicing intently—placing their hands at their sides, then shooting them up to their noses.

After everyone gets settled, three chairs are placed on the stage. Mayor Underwear sits in the first. Beside him is the only person from District 12 who's ever won the Hunger Games, Buttitch Totalapathy. From what I can tell, he's busy shouting to the gamblers in the front row. Next to Buttitch, and the first to the podium, is Effu Poorpeople. This awful woman serves as the liaison between the Capital and District 12 for the Hunger Games. Since she represents the Capital, she's very unpopular here. And like everyone from the Capital, she speaks in a strange accent.

"Welcome, everyone, to da Super Fun Day!" Effu says into the microphone. The Capital accent, I'm told, closely resembles what used to be called a "Jamaican" accent. "We gonna have a great time out here today!" Effu announces.

The moment is upon us. The nose game is about to start. Girls will go first. My heart is pounding. They're about to pick two kids who have to go far away, fight it out with a bunch of strangers, and face almost certain death. *Just make it quick*, I think. As long as it's not me, Prin, or Carol, I really don't care who the tributes are. I do hope it's that snotty brat Badge, though.

"Girls, are ya ready?" Effu scans the crowd to ensure all hands are down. Then, as is the custom, she says the slogan of the Hunger Games: "May da odds be eva in ya fava, mon!" The crowd grumbles back inaudibly. "All right, on ma signal. Ready, set, go!"

And with that, a thousand young hands shoot to their faces. From the back of the crowd, I can hear my mother blow her air horn. I've been practicing a lot lately and get my finger on my nose in record time. I'm a little off actually, so my finger goes up my nose, but it's there, nonetheless. I look around searching for the poor soul who came in last. Just then an image of a girl's face flashes up on the Jumbotron. The newest tribute from District 12.

It's Prin.

Crap.

This can't be happening. With my finger still stuffed deep up my nose, I spin around searching for Prin. I spot her a few yards away as she walks nervously toward the stage. Her eyes are wide with fear. The crowd groans. A young tribute like Prin doesn't stand much of a chance in the arena with older competitors. Plus, she's kind of ugly.

Suddenly, from behind me, I hear a shout. "I volunteer!" a voice cries. The crowd erupts in whispers as Effu raises the microphone to her lips.

"Who dat? Who wishes to volunteer for Prin Neverclean?" Effu asks.

To my surprise, the voice calls back, "I do—Kantkiss Neverclean!"

I'm stunned. Who said that? Who would volunteer *me*? *Maybe it's just someone else in the district with my exact same name*, I tell myself. That must be it. Just as I begin to relax again, I'm pushed and tugged toward the stage. No, the voice hasn't volunteered itself, it has volunteered me! I have been involuntarily volunteered!

I look back, scanning the crowd for the culprit. My eyes land on Slimey Sue. Her mouth is curled into a sinister smile. *It was her.* But why? Was it because I had forgotten her birthday? Or because I didn't return the spices I'd borrowed? Maybe it was because I accused her husband of a crime he didn't commit and he was subsequently executed. There is no way to know for sure. Whatever it was, Sue is still angry enough to fake my entry into the Hunger Games. It was probably the birthday thing.

With the entire crowd fixated on me, I briefly consider rescinding the offer, as it wasn't an offer I made to begin with. But then I think of poor little Prin and decide to take her place as tribute. I just hope she won't take the news too hard. I step forward.

"Yes!" Prin shouts out as she does a quick fist pump in the air. She gleefully hops down from the stage and rejoins her place in the crowd. Within seconds, she is back to giggling and chatting with her friends. *I'm sure she's hurting on the inside*, I tell myself as I walk toward the stage.

I reach the bottom of the steps and stare up at Effu. She extends a hand, dripping in diamonds, and I grab on tightly as I climb up beside her. "Ladies and gentlemen," Effu says regally in the Capital accent, "I'd like to present da first District Twelve volunteer in ova sixty years!"

Not one person in the crowd claps. It's dead silent. One person farts. To their credit, instead of applauding, the people of District 12 solemnly raise their hands in the air. Then, I watch as each person lifts a middle finger and flips the bird to Effu and the cameras.

Effu is enraged. "Put ya fingers down!" she shouts. "Put dem down now!" No one budges. "Very well. Our video editors gonna pixelate each and every one of ya hands." A loud groan emanates from the production crew's trailer.

I stare out over the crowd. I spot my mother, who is frantically waving a District 12 pennant and flashing me a big thumbs-up. I see Carol preparing for the male tribute to be selected. He's staring into a tiny handheld mirror, combing his hair and making kissing faces at himself.

As Effu prepares to signal the beginning of the male tribute selection, I take a seat beside Buttitch. He sizes me up for a moment, then opens his mouth to speak. "I've got a feeling about you, kid." For a second, I'm comforted. Then Buttitch turns toward the front of the crowd, where several gamblers and bookies have congregated. "I'd give her thirty to one odds," he yells. The gamblers commence a frenzy of shouting and toss around wads of cash. In addition to being known for winning the Hunger Games, Buttitch has a reputation for having a serious gambling addiction. He'll gamble on anything—the Hunger Games, weather, coin flips, traffic lights. He once bet his own grandmother she couldn't survive a whole week without her medication. And he was right.

"Hey, Buttitch!" One of the bookies is shouting up to him on the stage. At the podium, Effu is visibly irritated.

"Buttitch! We're putting the over-under on the girl's kills at two tributes. You want a piece of this action?"

"You bet I do!" Buttitch yells back. "Under!" He leaps out of his chair and heads toward the bookie. In his haste, Buttitch trips over the microphone wire and tumbles headfirst off the stage. He crashes into the ground with a loud thud. The crowd falls silent yet again, save for a few more farts.

While an ambulance crew hustles to tend to Buttitch, Effu announces the beginning of the male tribute selection. The cameras zoom in on the last boy to put his finger to his nose. I look up to the screen. I see a portly boy whose fingers are not on his nose but wrapped around a loaf of bread.

"Pita Malarkey!" Effu shouts.

My heart sinks. *Pita Malarkey.* I've heard this name before. Yes, when they took attendance for Super Fun Day like a half an hour ago. But even before that. Pita is my age and goes to school with me. His parents are bakers. And most important, Pita knew me at my most vulnerable moment.

Nearly three years have passed since my encounter with him. My father had just died in a freak explosion at the tele-marketing office. Mother, Prin, and I struggled to find food. At one point, I suggested that we eat Butterball, but Prin protested. "Just the tail, to see how he tastes," I offered. Prin remained firmly opposed. So I took it upon myself to get a job in the telemarketing office.

At work, I quickly distinguished myself as one of District 12's worst telemarketers. I smelled horrible, I didn't make any sales, and I spent most of my time stealing office supplies to trade in the Nob. One afternoon, after only two weeks on the job, my supervisor informed me that if I did not shape up, he would fire me. I promised to do better.

I sat down at my desk—or where my desk had been located before I stole it—and looked at the next name on my customer list. *Mr. Pumpernickel Malarkey*. The baker. I dialed his number.

"Hello?" said a gruff-sounding woman. It was Pumpernickel's wife, Sour Dough-Malarkey.

"Hi, ma'am. I'm Kantkiss, a representative with the District Twelve Call Catalog, and I'm wondering if you're interested in any of our new products, such as—"

She cut me off. "Do you want to order a cake, or what?" Mrs. Dough-Malarkey was not considered one of District 12's nicest citizens.

But before she could hang up, another voice came on the line.

"Mom, let me talk. We should order some more supplies for the store." This voice was different from Mrs. Dough-Malarkey's. It was soft and warm, like what a loaf of bread's voice would sound like. "Hi, I'm Pita Malarkey, Mr. Malarkey's son."

I knew him a bit from school. He was chubby and pale. He moved slowly and breathed laboriously. He also had a very large head. But beyond those flattering characteristics, I knew little about him.

"We'd like to order some cooking trays," he said.

And just like that, I had made a sale. Granted, we did not

sell cooking trays in the catalog, but my supervisor wouldn't uncover this discrepancy for another week. By that time, I had made a few more sales. In one small moment, Pita had given me the confidence to be a moderately successful telemarketer. My paycheck grew to be enough to support Mother and Prin, and I supplemented it with plenty of hunting on the side. We were back on track, thanks to the Boy with the Head.

Now, as I stand on stage in the public square, Pita walks toward me with his giant head hung low. When he reaches the stairs to the stage, he struggles to climb them, stopping every few steps to catch his breath. He's really out of shape. At one point he sits down, sweat dripping down his face. After about thirty seconds of rest, he proceeds and ascends the fourth and final stair to the stage.

"District Twelve!" shouts Effu. "Meet ya tributes!"

Aside from the gamblers, who are nearly hysterical, the crowd reacts glumly to Pita and me. Mayor Underwear strides over to the podium and thanks Effu. He is about to recite the Oath of Loyalty. It's required that each district's mayor read it annually at Super Fun Day. It's Capital propaganda and the people hate it. From a few feet away, I can hear him whispering to himself before he begins. "Okay, Underwear. You got this. You practiced all week. You didn't even do your other work, you just practiced. That work was really important; you shouldn't have neglected it. But you did. So take a few deep breaths, and do this right. They're going to love you."

As soon as he begins speaking, he is met with a chorus of boos. In accordance with Capital law, he must continue. I feel slightly bad for Mayor Underwear, before I remember the peril of my own situation. I hardly listen and only realize my mind has wandered when the Oath is finished. For most of District 12, Super Fun Day has concluded. The citizens all head home, except for the homeless ones, who mill around the square for a few minutes before selecting a place to sit down.

A few Pacemakers escort me over to the Injustice Building, where I am placed in a lavishly decorated room. It has a glimmering chandelier, a bearskin carpet, and a sofa. I have never seen a sofa before. At first, I lie down underneath it. That doesn't seem right. Then I stand behind it for a while. Close, but definitely not what a sofa is for. Finally, I figure out how it works. When Effu walks in a minute later, I'm straddling one of the sofa's arms like I'm riding a horse. As I teeter back and forth, knocking over an end table, Effu tells me that for the next hour, I will receive visitors who have come to say their good-byes before I depart for the Capital.

Prin and my mother are the first to arrive. Mother is ecstatic. "Can you believe this is actually where the tributes say good-bye every year?" She snaps a few pictures with a disposable camera. "Buttitch Totalapathy probably sat in that very same chair!"

Prin is less enthusiastic. She keeps glancing at the clock on the wall. I can tell that this is difficult for her. She's really going to miss me.

"Get away from me!" she shrieks, as I try to pull her in for a hug. "Mom, Kantkiss won't stop touching me!" Prin is so adorable. I know she's just trying to be brave.

"Kantkiss," my mother says, "promise me one thing." I know what's coming. She's going to ask me to promise that I'll do my best to survive. That no matter how tough it gets in the arena, no matter how desperate and violent the situation may seem, I must try to make it. "Promise me that you will get the president's autograph."

Before I can respond, Prin is tugging on my mother's shirt. "Can we get out of here?"

"Oh, all right," my mother says. She takes a few last photos. "Kantkiss," she says from behind the camera, "get out of the way, you're blocking the sofa." After the flash goes off, she heads for the door. "Remember: autograph."

As they disappear out the door, I begin to wonder whether I'll ever see them again. But within seconds, my next visitor arrives. I'm surprised to see that it's Pita's father, Pumpernickel Malarkey. I've dealt with him in the market and at his bakery, but I can't fathom what he'd be doing here on Super Fun Day. Shouldn't he be visiting his own son?

"Hi, Kantkiss. I just wanted to come wish you good luck," he says, pulling a neatly wrapped package from his coat. "I also wanted to give you these cookies." He hands me the package. *What an incredibly nice gesture*, I think to myself. Even though I might kill his son on national television in a few days, he's treating me with kindness. "Finally," he adds, "I want you to know that Pita is a very slow runner, and his most vulnerable points are his stomach and his crotch." What a kind man!

Pumpernickel exits the room, and just as I'm about to climb atop the sofa again, his wife, Mrs. Sour Dough-Malarkey, bursts through the door. "Give me those!" she shouts, prying the cookies from my hands. Then she leaves.

My next visitor is less surprising. Carol glides into the room like an angel. He approaches the sofa like an expert and sits down on its cushion. "Ohhh," I say. I take a seat beside him. Carol begins to speak. He's talking about perseverance and survival, but I'm too distracted by his beautiful mouth and his perfect nose to listen to a word he says. His deep, dark eyes look so concerned. I can't process a single sentence while looking at them.

A few minutes pass and Carol stands up to leave. I'm jolted back to attention. "Anyway, as long as you do that, I think you should be fine," he says. I quickly nod my head in agreement. Just as I begin to fault myself for not listening, I lose myself gazing at Carol's amazing butt as he strolls out of the room as smoothly as he arrived.

Badge Underwear, the mayor's daughter, walks through the door just after Carol's exit. "Kantkiss, I want you to know that you're my best friend and I'll be cheering for you," she says. I'm shocked because I don't really have any friends, and I definitely don't like Badge. But before I tell her this, the gold pin on her dress catches my eye.

"Badge? Since you're my best friend and all, then you wouldn't mind giving me your pin, would you?" I bat my eyelashes a few times to look sweet.

"My pin? Oh, of course, Kantkiss! I'd be honored if you'd wear it." She removes it from her dress and hands it to me.

"Right—*wear it*," I say. *I'm going to sell this thing the first chance I get*, I think to myself.

Badge says a quick good-bye. Unexpectedly, one more person walks into the room to see me. It's Mrs. Davis, my schoolteacher. She drops a pile of papers into my lap. "Here's the homework for the days you'll be missing," she says. Then, like those before her, Mrs. Davis heads for the door. Effu pokes her head in the room.

"It's time to go to da Capital!" she shrieks.

"Nobody else has come to say good-bye?" I ask.

"Nope. Congratulations, ya had da fewest visitors in Hunger Games history," Effu says.

We walk over to the train station to board a high-speed train. On the platform, I see Pita. His eyes are wet with tears and he's drying them with a baguette. We're ushered into the same plush compartment as the train's engines spring to life.

In school, they tell us that the Capital is built in a region once called "California." District 12 is in an area formerly known as "Cleveland." They also teach us about how that world ended and how Peaceland began, but I zone out a lot in class so I can't really remember. Sorry if you wanted to know about that part.

Effu beckons me and Pita to a dinner in the train's dining car. When I walk in, I'm speechless. The table is covered with more food than I've ever seen in my entire life. Bacon cheeseburgers, chili dogs, nachos, french fries, and General Tso's chicken are spread across the table on large platters.

Pita begins to hyperventilate. I plant my face right into the pile of burgers. It's heavenly. It tastes even better than the finest squirrel meat.

Using my hands, I shovel food into my mouth until I'm stuffed. I wipe my mouth on the tablecloth, but once it's drenched in sauce, I begin wiping my mouth on Effu's shirtsleeve. Effu is disgusted. "Each year, da tributes' manners are worse den da year before," she says. While she complains, Pita blows his nose into a hamburger bun. Effu dry-heaves for a few seconds before beginning to speak. "Ya need ta be on ya best behavior for da sponsors," she says. "Dis won't do."

Effu's right. We have to consider how we look to the sponsors. Sponsors are an important part of the Hunger Games. They can deliver gifts of supplies to tributes while they're in the arena. Receiving a sponsorship gift can make the difference between life and death.

The door slides open and Buttitch walks in. "Effu, can you spot me a few hundred dollars?" he asks.

Effu tosses her napkin onto the table and gets up from her seat. "No, Buttitch!" she shouts, leaving the room.

Buttitch takes her seat at the table. Before Pita can stop him, he grabs the hamburger bun from Pita's plate and takes a large bite. "Hm, didn't know they put mayonnaise on these," he says, as he finishes it off.

As a former Hunger Games champion—also known as a *serial killer*—Buttitch will coach Pita and me throughout the competition. His coaching record is an encouraging 0–24.

Many people in District 12 think his gambling addiction is to blame for his poor performance.

"Do either of you have some money I can borrow?" Buttitch asks. "I'll get it back to you. I'll double it. It's a sure thing." Pita and I shake our heads. "Too bad," he says. "Look, I don't have a whole lot of time to talk—I'm betting the conductor that he can't go twice the speed limit without derailing the train—but I just want to say a few words of advice for when we arrive."

Pita and I lean in to listen. "When we get to the Capital," he says, "eat at O'Doyle's. It's the best pub in the city. Great buffalo wings." This hardly seems useful, but when I glance at Pita, he's hurriedly writing "O'Doyle's wings" on the back of his hand. "And just as important," Buttitch continues, "listen to your stylists."

Just then, the train starts to slow down. I look out the window. We're already pulling into the Capital. The train is cruising up Main Street in the shadow of a magnificent castle, steepled with spires and surrounded by a large moat. We pass the faded image of a cartoon mouse wearing white gloves. Buttitch tells us a bit about the city. "There are a few distinct neighborhoods. Over there is Tomorrowland, and that over there is Epcot." He's pointing out the window. "And there's the Training Center." We've arrived.

Ouch!" I cry as another strip of wax is peeled off, taking the last of my lower-back hair with it.

"Cool it, mon," shouts Venereal, one of my assistant stylists. Like Effu, she speaks with the strange Capital accent, drawing out the letters into sounds I've never heard before. "Ya got bear fur back here! Relax, we almost done. Now roll over to ya backside."

I feel tired, as I didn't sleep well in the train station's motel last night. The bed was too soft and clean.

I'm lying in the middle of a cold room filled with cosmetic supplies and mirrors. This is where my stylists will give me a makeover and costume for the Opening Ceremony. They're a strange bunch, my stylists. Like all Capital residents, their speech, fashions, and mannerisms are like nothing I've ever encountered.

Another assistant, Flabbiest, sits in the corner stroking his cosmetic horns. He stands and walks over. "You always do da waxin'," he complains to Venereal.

"Well, maybe if ya had both arms, ya'd be half as good as me," Venereal says. It's true, Flabbiest, in keeping with this season's fashions, has no left arm. It's been deliberately lopped off at the shoulder. Although it seems peculiar, even in District 12 we are amazed by the beautiful asymmetry of what we call the *amputistas* filling television talk shows and runways.

I hope they don't chop off my arm, I think to myself, shivering in the cold. I'm completely naked. A blank slate for the styling team to work with.

Flabbiest begins to spread cream all over my face. "Chin up, missy. We gonna shave ya whiskers," he says.

As his razor begins shearing away long wisps of my facial hair, I think about how in the Crack it's a mark of strength for a woman to have a few proud whiskers. When I sit up, clean-shaven, the last assistant, Octopus, nods in approval. Her smile reveals how fashion savvy she really is: she has no teeth.

"Dat does it," Flabbiest says. He sounds pleased with his work. "We've gotten rid of da coarsest hair, removed da fungus and moles, and treated ya scoliosis. We even fixed ya breasts, so now dey're da same size."

"Thanks," I say, trying to appear sweet and grateful. I remember Buttitch's advice. I'll have enough enemies once the Hunger Games begin. It wouldn't hurt to have the stylists on my side. They seem to be falling for my nice-girl act, so I keep it going. "We don't have much reason back home to look pretty," I tell them. Then I pinch my own cheek and giggle.

The assistants squeal with delight. They understand that I've had a rough upbringing living outside the Capital.

"Don't get me started on dis government!" Octopus says. "Did ya see what President Bernette was wearin' last year at the Openin' Ceremony? Dat pinstripe suit? He looked like a real cockatoo!"

Just then the door bursts open and a squadron of Pace-makers dressed in black marches in. They grab Octopus and drag her outside.

Venereal clears her throat. "All right, dear, thas enough for today. Now that ya look like a normal, healthy human, Cinnabon can finally have a look at ya." At last, I will get to meet *the* stylist.

She and Flabbiest gather their supplies and exit the room. Once they're gone, I remember that I'm naked. It didn't bother me in front of the assistants. For one thing, I appreciated the attention. And I'm pretty sure they were naked too. It was very hard to tell with all their tattoos and extragenital accessories.

The door slides open, not at all like the doors back in District 12, which are mostly just tarps. In walks an old man, dressed in a green canvas smock, fashionably holding a bucket. He studies my naked body. I know it's crucial to stay perfectly still to show I trust his judgment.

After about four minutes of this, I can't hold out any longer. I blurt out, "You're not like any stylist I've ever seen on TV."

"Stylist? I'm just the janitor," the man says. "I had to see for myself what kind of creature was shedding all the hair and fur I've been shoveling into the furnace. My guess was a wolf, maybe a moose." I cover my chest, embarrassed. "Anyway, nice to meet you. My name's Barnels." He gives my body one last look from top to bottom and then hobbles back outside.

After that I lose track of time. Back in District 12, few are rich enough to afford clocks, so if we need to know the time, we walk to the public square and ask Counting Richard, a man who spends all day counting.

Just as I begin to doze off for a quick naked nap, an exquisitely stylish man steps into the room. His hair is dashing—business in the front, party in the back. He wears a Hawaiian shirt, buttoned crookedly and untucked from his cargo shorts. On his feet, lime green Crocs. The ensemble takes my breath away.

"Hi, I'm Cinnabon, your stylist for the Hunger Games. You must be . . ." He unfolds a piece of paper from his pocket. "Terry."

"It's Kantkiss," I say.

"Right!" he says. "Terry was last year's tribute. God rest his soul."

I bow my head in respect.

Cinnabon breaks the silence. "You must be hungry," he says. With his finger, he presses a button on his chair that says Fancy Lunch Button. A meal instantly falls into the room from the ceiling. I notice that Cinnabon doesn't speak with the Capital accent.

I eye the food excitedly. "Wait!" Cinnabon yells before I can dig in. "For the love of Bernette, put some clothes on before you start gorging yourself. I don't know if the naked thing is a custom in your district or just a personal preference, but either way you need to cover up all that back stubble if I'm going to have any chance of keeping my food down."

After I throw on a robe, we eat. The food is amazing. Cinnabon's lunch is served on fine china. He eats a steak dusted in rosemary atop wild rice, with pudding for dessert. And for me, on the carpet, is a tray of steamed cabbage, an assortment of different roots, a full corncob, all mashed together with chicken neck. We have nothing this delicious back home, and though my heart is full of hate toward the Capital, my belly is full of yum-yums.

Cinnabon puts down his fork. "You must think we're all monsters," he says. His eyes glare at me and I feel my breathing quicken. I'm not sure if I should answer, or nod, or stay silent, or try a cartwheel. Unsure of how to proceed, I let out a burp.

Cinnabon nods understandingly and continues. "It must seem so awful: fat, rich Capital residents snatching up half-fed, mangy children so they can watch them slaughter one another." Cinnabon has surprised me, both by his cold assessment of the Hunger Games and by starting his meal with the pudding. "Anyway, about your costume."

My costume. This is the part I've been dreading, even more than my probable death alone in the wilderness. For the Opening Ceremony, tributes are dressed in a costume representing their districts, and since District 12 is the telemarketing district, our tributes usually end up looking like phone books.

"Now, I could've sworn the Hunger Games didn't start until next week," Cinnabon says, as he picks up a small suitcase from beside his chair. "I must have misread my calendar. But I did my best to throw something together at the last minute. Don't worry, nobody will notice that it was rushed."

Cinnabon reaches a hand into the suitcase and pulls out a large white sheet. He unfurls it and holds it up for me to see. It's just a regular sheet, aside from two small holes cut in the middle. Cinnabon tosses the sheet over himself and twists and turns until his eyes are visible through the holes. "You'll be a ghost!" he declares.

At first, I don't say anything. I stare blankly at the ghost standing before me. I take a moment and walk a full circle around Cinnabon. "Well?" he says from beneath the sheet. "What do you think?"

"It's . . . it's . . . genius!" I say. Cinnabon shimmies out of the sheet and tosses it over me. It fits perfectly. He can't see it, but I'm ecstatic. I've never felt so beautiful.

I'm rushed downstairs for the ceremony. Everyone we pass in the halls jumps back in horror before realizing I'm not a real ghost. Then they congratulate Cinnabon on his masterpiece. At this year's Emmy Awards, Cinnabon will be a lock for Best Costume Design, Reality Series.

Finally, we arrive at the child stable where the tributes are kept until the ceremony begins. Pita walks in a few minutes later. His costume is beautiful. His doughy body is enclosed in a hulking black plastic suit meant to replicate a Singer-Point 14 series telephone—just like the one they use back home in the telemarketing office. As I stare at Pita, he keeps trying to scratch an itch on his butt, which involves slapping the 9 button with his palm.

I go over to Pita to ask him about his experience with the stylists. "That was pretty weird, huh?" I say. "Especially being naked in front of all those strangers."

"You were naked?" Pita says.

"Yeah. Wasn't everybody?" I say.

Pita shakes his head. "I didn't get naked," he says. In the hallway, a few other tributes shake their heads as well.

A couple guards walk in and push us into the front of the child stable, from which we'll enter the stadium for the Opening Ceremony. Attached to a chariot stand two massive horses. I've never seen a horse up close before. They're extremely rare in the woods of District 12, and I've been dying to hunt one since I was a little girl.

One by one, the different tribute pairs will emerge from the child stable onto the stadium floor. Tributes will ride their chariots toward the center of the stadium, where a large stage awaits.

The first tributes to ride out are from District 1. District 1 is known as the champions district. Whereas my district specializes in telemarketing, District 1 specializes in breeding kids to dominate the Hunger Games. These kids are big, strong, and ruthless. They ride out wearing varsity letter jackets and drinking Red Bull.

District 2 is next. District 2 is the ultimate fighting district, and it's home to some vicious kids. Its tributes are wearing basketball shorts, tattoos, and mohawks. Even in the chariot, they're kicking and punching each other, entertaining the audience as they inflict pain. Like District 1 tributes, tributes from the ultimate fighting district usually do very well in the Hunger Games.

The districts roll by, too many for me to possibly count. I catch the girl tribute from District 7, the district attorney district, staring at me contemptuously. I can tell that beneath her pantsuit there is a fierce rage directed straight at me, although I have no idea why. Maybe it's my killer costume that's setting her off.

The next pair is from District 8, the red light district. I'm not sure what they make there, but their tributes are dressed very provocatively.

Later comes District 10, the theater district, and as usual both tributes are boys.

By counting my fingers and toes, I conclude that our turn is coming up. Pita and I mount our chariot. As we move into view of the crowd, and the millions of viewers across Peaceland, I feel sick with nervousness. *Man, I hope they like my outfit.*

"Boooo! Boooo!" the crowd screams in an obvious nod to my ghost costume. On the Jumbotron, Cinnabon's face appears. The crowd stops booing and goes absolutely wild. Cinnabon is one of the most popular stylists, and everything he's associated with is a hit. My white sheet is no exception. Even though Cinnabon is burying his head in his hands, I know that he's proud of us. The crowd chants his name.

Our chariot comes to a stop at the broad semicircle formed by all the tributes. Taken together, the costumes are truly magnificent. Pita and I are the capstone: telephone and ghost. President Mark Bernette appears at the podium and the crowd erupts in applause. He raises a hand to indicate that he'd like the crowd to quiet down. Immediately, there is silence. No farts.

Good afternoon," bellows President Bernette. "Welcome to the Seventy-Fourth Hunger Games."

As I process that statement, I realize its magnitude: I am one of a long line of telemarketing district tributes. I am being welcomed. And there have been at least fifty Hunger Games before this one.

President Bernette grips the podium firmly with both hands. He is a good-looking man, with a wide forehead, flowing brown hair, and a dashing smile that he never flashes. He wears a black suit with a black dress shirt underneath. His boxers, I've been told, are also black. When I look at him the only color I find is in his rosy cheeks.

He continues. "We know there are three keys to a healthy society: having elected leaders, promoting separation of powers, and making children fight to the death on national TV."

The crowd roars in agreement. Pita claps also. I don't blame him. He's simply distracted by the bagel he's pulled from his pocket, completely unaware of what's been said.

"To suppress a revolution," President Bernette goes on, "it's important to infuriate and humiliate your constituents regularly, while televising the deaths of their children. On that note, I am happy to welcome these fine tributes. We have a great arena prepared this year, and it should be fun to watch them die—not like that one year where they all starved to death and it took forever."

The crowd applauds. Pita, listening now, looks appropriately concerned. The Boy with the Head and I exchange worried looks.

"Seeing as how these games are quite perilous, I would like to remind the tributes that you are free to leave at any time," President Bernette says.

Phew! Pita and I smile. That's great news. I imagine Prin watching this. I miss her so much. And I imagine my mother beside her—that stupid woman. I think of them hearing this and realizing that I can come home safely. Maybe Pita and I will leave tomorrow. Or we'll enjoy touring the Capital for a few more days. I breathe a sigh of relief, knowing that I will soon be back home, living in horrible poverty.

President Bernette repeats himself. "That's right, you can leave the arena at any time and go back ho—" An adviser cuts him off and whispers in his ear. After nodding, President Bernette continues. "Sorry, sorry, I was thinking of something else," he says. "Sorry about that." He laughs. "You can only leave if you die."

Pita and I look at each other again. We go back to being scared.

"In closing," President Bernette says, his voice sonorous, his hair gelled, his views right-wing, "I hope you have enjoyed these Opening Ceremonies. To the tributes, I hope you take pride in a few things: your district, getting to be on live TV, and the fact that you will die in interesting ways. Enjoy the evening. Remember, the food court closes at ten thirty."

Now that the ceremony is over, Pita and I ride our chariot back to the Training Center. Pita wants to stop at a drive-thru, but I remind him that Effu asked us to be in the apartment for dinner. To show his frustration, Pita tries to cross his arms, but he can't. He settles for making a pouty face.

On the ride to the Training Center, we pass Buttitch huddled with a group of men on a street corner. They're exchanging money and slips of paper. I can tell that they're making bets on the Hunger Games. When Buttitch spots us, he hurriedly puts away the money. The others follow suit. Then, in an effort to look casual, they all start whistling and walking in small circles.

As I walk into the training center, I try not to think about how my life is basically in Buttitch's hands. This building is amazing. It has a floor for each district. I step into a thing Effu calls an "elevator." When you get out, you are at a different place than you were when you got in. Unless you do not press a button. The whole experience is remarkable. The only other times I've ever been in an elevator were when I went to the District 12 Injustice Building to collect my father's vaporized body, and every day at school when I rode the elevator to class.

As I ride this elevator, I remember the year that the Hunger Games took place in an arena that was made to resemble an office building. Most of the tributes from poor districts were decapitated by elevators because they weren't familiar with them. Man, those were good Hunger Games.

I step off the elevator and into the apartment. Like the compartment on the train, it's very deluxe. Pita sits down to take off his sneakers. *Good idea*, I think. This is a nice place; we should remove our dirty footwear. But then I see that he's just getting some crackers out of his shoes. As he pulls a few up to his mouth, Effu slaps them out of his hand. "Don't spoil ya dinna!"

I excuse myself and head for the bathroom. When I shut the door behind me, I let out a deep breath, pleased to have a moment alone for the first time since Super Fun Day. I look around the bathroom. Nothing is familiar. There's a silver tube that pees water. There's a bar of a thing called "soap." The toilet has a lever that makes water disappear counterclockwise and then reappear again. I use the toilet and, for the first time in my life, enjoy pooping without digging a hole first.

When I walk out, Effu is standing there waiting for me. "Here," she says, handing me a small matchbox. "Ya betta light a match in there."

"Is that a Capital custom?" I ask.

"No. It's not," she says, pinching her nose.

I do as she says, and then we head toward the dining

room. There, I find another massive meal. Pizza, mozzarella sticks, Diet Coke, McFlurries, lobsters, Polish meatballs, pretzels, Swedish meatballs, and a giant tub of raw cookie dough. *Mmm.* I lick my lips. Then I lick my hands: this is how we wash our hands in District 12. I take a seat at the table next to Pita. Effu, Buttitch, and Cinnabon join us.

We start eating. "Did you know this year you can actually bet on the order that the tributes die?" Buttitch says. "I've been advocating that for years. Finally!"

Cinnabon looks worried.

"I've got you going fourth," Buttitch says excitedly, pointing his knife toward Pita. "Dying fourth, I mean. Kantkiss— you'll go sixth. Now, I want—"

"That's enough!" Cinnabon says, cutting him off.

"You're right." Buttitch nods. "I'd better not jinx it."

When I'm about halfway through my first plateful of meatballs, I think about how long it would take me to assemble this meal at home. For the McFlurries, I'd just hit up McDonald's. But for the meat, I'd have to kill at least two cows. One for the meat and the other for sport. Then I'd have to kill about a dozen squirrels to trade for the other foods. For the pizza, Carol and I would have to search the woods all day for tomatoes and a pizza oven.

Buttitch, his mouth full of cookie dough, begins to reminisce about past Hunger Games. "Five or six years ago, little Gary Schechter, he put up a good fight. Made District Twelve proud. Like many District Twelve tributes before him, it all ended when he got his intestines ripped out."

Pita and I swallow our food hard. It's not pleasant to hear about our predecessors.

"Had a nice funeral, though. Real nice. Flowers, band, speeches," Buttitch says.

I try not to listen.

He keeps talking. "Herbert Morton—*that* was a funeral. After he was eaten by another tribute in the Hunger Games ten years ago, they buried what was left of him in the most magnificent pearl casket."

"Quit talking about funerals, Buttitch! You'll frighten the kids," Cinnabon says.

I'm grateful to have Cinnabon here. He seems like a real friend.

"It's insensitive," Cinnabon remarks. "Everyone knows they don't have funerals for dead tributes anymore."

When we start to run low on mozzarella sticks, a red-haired girl emerges from the kitchen with a new tray. She looks familiar and vaguely reminds me of someone I betrayed one time. While Effu and Buttitch talk, I can't stop staring at this girl. Then it hits me.

"I know you!" I say to the girl.

Everyone at the table gets quiet and stares at me. The girl glances at me for a second, then walks quickly back to the kitchen. "Hey!" I shout at her. But she's disappeared behind the door. I try to remember where I know her from. The market? The Capital? This dinner?

"How could you possibly know a Notalks?" Cinnabon asks.

"A what?" I reply.

"A Notalks," he says. "Someone who has committed a crime. The Capital cuts off their tongues as punishment."

"Ya couldn't possibly know her," Effu says.

"I'll bet she does know her," Buttitch says excitedly. "What's it worth to you?" He takes out a fistful of cash. "One hundred? Two hundred? I'm not going higher than three hundred. All right, three-fifty!"

While he rambles on, it finally clicks. I remember how I know the Notalks.

Effu shakes her head. "No gambling, Buttitch!" She turns to me. "So, where do ya know dis girl from?"

Before I can say anything, Pita comes to my rescue. "She looks just like"—Pita's glancing nervously around the room and then he continues—"Dietcoke Elevatortable!"

"Yes, Dietcoke Elevatortable," I say confidently. Pita's trying to protect me. Very clever.

"Dietcoke is this girl at our school," Pita says. "I noticed that the Notalks looked familiar too, but I just couldn't put my finger on it. It's clear now, though. She's the spitting image of Dietcoke."

Both Effu and Cinnabon shrug. They appear convinced. I breathe a sigh of relief. I'm not sure why Pita would try to protect me. His behavior can only be interpreted as an effort to kill me. It couldn't be that he's just a nice guy.

Everybody continues feasting on dinner. Pita eats more lobster at this meal than I'd eat in a month back home. The only time he stops shoveling food into his mouth is when he starts choking. Each time this happens, Buttitch calmly gets up and gives him the Heimlich.

As the Notalks comes out of the kitchen to refill the platters in front of Pita, I notice that she keeps flashing me mean looks. Could it be possible that she's still mad at me?

After we finish dinner, the adults clear the table. Buttitch moves his chair closer to Pita and me. "Okay, guys, training starts tomorrow," he says. "As you train, be sure to showcase your skills. The Rainmakers will be watching."

The Rainmakers are the people who design the Hunger Games. They determine everything from the arena location to the weather to the jacket on the special edition Hunger Games DVD that will come out when it's all over. It's important to impress them.

"Kantkiss, I hear you're pretty good with a bow and arrow," Buttitch says. "Pita," he continues, "I hear you're a nice guy." Pita stares at Buttitch, waiting for more concrete praise. "Well, good night," Buttitch says, standing to his feet.

When he leaves the room, Pita turns to me. "So, Dietcoke Elevatortable?" he says, smiling.

"We can't talk here," I say, eyeing the poorly hidden cameras in the walls. There's a print of Leonardo da Vinci's *Mona Lisa* hanging to our left with two giant lenses protruding from the eyes. "Let's talk on the roof."

We hop into the elevator and, unsure of how to go up, press all the buttons. Before we get to the roof, the elevator doors slide open on a handful of other floors, offering us a glimpse of a few other tributes. On the seventh floor, the tributes from District 7—the district attorney district—are proofing legal briefs before bed. On the ninth floor, the tributes from District 9 are curled up on a couch watching the movie *District 9*. Then, on ten, we see the tributes from the theater district doing voice exercises. "Me-mi-ma-mo-moo!" they sing on an upward scale, "I'm-going-to-kill-you!"

Finally, we reach the roof. The moment we step off the elevator into the wind, I see something unexpected. Buttitch is a few feet away, standing on a ledge like he's about to jump off the building. It's loud, but I can make out parts of what he's muttering to himself: "Just do it, man . . . So much debt! . . . Stop being such a wuss and jump . . . Come on, get it over with . . . I'm going to jump!"

"Buttitch!" I scream, rushing toward him.

He spins around. "Hello, children," he says glumly. "What are you doing up here?"

"What are *we* doing up here?" Pita asks. "What are *you* doing up there?"

Buttitch scratches the back of his head and shifts nervously. "Well, to be honest, I'm in a lot of gambling debt. I don't see how I'm going to pay it all off. This seemed like my best option."

Pita nods and backs away, convinced that Buttitch is right. He gestures that I should do the same. "Pita—no. Get down from there, Buttitch!" I scream.

"Why should I?" he says.

"Because you have so much to live for!" I yell. "And we need your help to make it out of the Hunger Games alive."

Buttitch peers over the ledge. It's a long way down. He takes a deep breath, then steps back onto the roof. Without saying a word, he walks over to me and, for a moment, puts his hand on my shoulder. Then he gets into the elevator and goes back downstairs.

"That was intense," I say to Pita. Judging by his pit stains, he agrees.

We find a bench to sit on while we talk. From there, we enjoy a breathtaking view of the Capital. We can see all the way up Main Street and even over to the Animal Kingdom. And despite the wind, I can hear Capital residents shriek with delight as they ride the spinning teacups near the bottom of the building.

"So tell me," Pita says, "how do you know the Notalks?"

I tell the story. It was about six months ago. I was in the woods hunting with Carol when I saw them. The girl from dinner was in the bushes with a boy. From what I could tell, they were kissing. I didn't like that one bit. There I was, trying to hunt, and they're scaring away all the animals with their loud smooching. So I called the Pacemakers on them. They showed up and captured those two lovebirds and arrested them for trespassing. How was I supposed to know the punishment for French kissing was that you get your tongue cut out?

"Wow," Pita says once I've finished, "she must be awfully mad at you."

"Nah, it was so long ago," I assure him. "By now, she's probably gotten used to living without a tongue and as a slave."

Pita starts shivering in the cold and says he wants to go inside. With all that blubber on his bones, I know he's only pretending to be cold and that he really just wants to go downstairs to eat more. But I'm ready to go to sleep, so I go anyway.

I bid Pita good night in the hallway outside my bedroom. When I step inside, the Notalks is there waiting for me. She's drawn the sheets back on my bed, and she's holding a warm glass of milk for me. *Would somebody who's still mad at me be this nice?* I think to myself reassuringly. Then I watch as the Notalks clears her throat and spits into the milk. *That was probably an accident,* I tell myself as I climb into the soft bed.

"So, how long have you been working here?" I ask the Notalks. She glares at me. "Right, you can't speak. Sorry," I say. An awkward silence follows. "Do you enjoy the work?" No response. She points angrily at her mouth. "That was a yes-or-no question, you could have answered it," I tell her. Her face starts to get red.

I decide I'd better be a little nicer to the Notalks. I stand up next to her and take her hand. I look right into her eyes. "What's your name?" I ask.

For the first time since I've seen her, the angry look disappears from her face. She walks over to the windowsill, where there's a vase holding a single rose. She raises a finger and points at it.

"That's lovely. But what's your name?" I ask.

She points at the rose again.

"What? You want me to water it? Isn't that your job?" I say.

She points again, more emphatically.

"Oh! Your name! Your name is . . . vase?"

She shakes her head, then starts circling the rose with her hand.

"Circle! Your name is Circle!"

The Notalks buries her face in her hands for a moment, then lifts the rose out of the vase.

"All right, Circle, you can have the rose. But everything else in this room belongs to me," I say, as I climb back into bed. "Now tuck me in."

Circle sighs deeply and approaches the bed. She pulls the sheets up over me nice and tight. Then she takes a pillow and pushes it over my face, hard. I start to giggle.

"Hey, cut that out, you'll suffocate me!" I say between laughs. She finally relents. I sit up, gasping for air. "So what did they do with your tongue after they cut it out? Did you get to keep it?"

The Notalks furrows her brow, then snatches the vase from the other side of the room. *We're getting along great*, I think to myself. *There's no way she could still be mad at me.* As I pepper Circle with more questions, she raises the vase high up in the air. Then, to help me fall asleep immediately, she slams it down on my head and knocks me unconscious.

The next morning, I awake with a headache. I swing my feet down onto the floor and recoil in pain. I cut my feet on bits of glass. The vase is mysteriously shattered on the floor. I groggily walk over to the closet, where I find an outfit has already been picked out for me. I'm happy to see it's my usual attire: black pants, maroon tunic, lace bra, and frilly panties.

I go into the dining room. The table is practically empty, aside from a giant stack of pancakes, a tray of bacon, and a platter of scrambled eggs. I sigh loudly. Could the Hunger Games get *any* worse? I'm sick of eating all these expensive meals and living rent-free in a luxury apartment. I just wish I could go home to my shack.

Buttitch steps into the room. I notice that he enters from the front door, rather than from his bedroom.

"Have you been out all night?" I ask.

He grunts affirmatively, grabbing a handful of bacon as he passes through the room. Before he leaves, he says, "Be sure to stick with Pita today. The two of you will fare much better if you're together." Then he's gone.

I busy myself with breakfast, but I can't help but think about Pita. He's been acting strange lately. Buttitch wants us to act like friends, but I've never had any friends so I'm not sure what to do. Pita's been doing his best to play the part. He compliments me all the time. He writes me romantic sonnets. And when I have to step in puddles, he lays himself down in the water so I can walk on his back to avoid getting wet. You know, normal friend stuff.

Just as I'm thinking of him, Pita walks into the room. He's still in his pajamas and he's chewing on a pretzel.

"You'd better get dressed. We'll be late for training," I say.

"All right, just give me one second," he says. He goes into the kitchen for a moment and returns with a burlap sack. Then he positions the sack at the edge of the table and holds it open. "Do me a favor, Kantkiss. Push all the food into this sack."

Once his food sack is full, Pita scurries off to get his clothes. Then we hop in the elevator and ride all the way down to the training level. When we arrive, we join the group of tributes already standing in the middle of the gymnasium floor.

As the head trainer explains the day's schedule, I examine the other tributes. Some look like the type of kids you'd find back in District 12. They're thin and pale. But others— the Varsity tributes—look big and tough. They're trained in combat, as well as screen presence, in the hopes of one day winning the Hunger Games and ultimately getting a starring role on a major network sitcom. Indeed, most champions get a show for a few years before the public grows tired of them. Growing up, I can remember watching *Buttitch Totalapathy, MD* with my father.

But for every Varsity tribute that's here today, there are thousands more at home who *weren't* selected to participate in the Hunger Games. I shudder when I think about those kids. All their lives, they grow up training for the Hunger Games. They do nothing but throw spears and practice decapitating people. Then, at the age of eighteen, they must immediately forget all that and transition to being normal. All of a sudden, they're not killing machines, they're tax attorneys. Or chefs. Tragically, many end up as *unheralded* murderers.

One of the Varsities gathers the rest around him in a huddle. He kneels in the center and addresses them. "All right, you guys, this is it. The big day. So let's go out there and give it all we've got," he shouts. "We've been waiting our whole lives for this. Savor this moment," he adds with a grin. When the huddle breaks up, the boy sees that I'm looking at him. He glares at me. From the Opening Ceremony, I know his name. Archie Nemesis. Something tells me that the two of us aren't going to get along. As I return his death stare, I notice that Pita is waving frantically at Archie. I elbow him in the stomach.

"Ow!" Pita says. "What'd you do that for?"

"Quit waving at Archie," I tell him. "He's probably going to kill us both!"

Pita rubs his stomach. "I don't know," he says, "seems like a pretty cool guy to me."

Next to Archie, I see a girl tribute. She's roughly my age and she's clinging to Archie, petting his firm biceps. Her hair is long and blond. She's beautiful. From the looks of it, I doubt they had to shave much of her facial hair during her makeover. She probably didn't have much to begin with.

"That's Mandy. Mandy Kappagamma." Pita says, gazing at her. "Man, I hope we're the last two left."

I elbow him in the stomach again.

From across the room, I can hear Mandy whisper to another girl tribute. She's talking about Archie. "I *think* he likes me, but I'm also, like, *sooo* worried he's going to, like, *murder* me or something because of this whole 'only one can survive' thing. I don't know, I'm probably just overthinking it."

With the blow of a whistle, the head trainer announces the start of training. We have the next few hours to visit skill stations where we can practice for our time in the arena. I look around at our options. Among them, I see a spear-throwing station, a wine-tasting station, and a train station.

"Well, where should we go first?" Pita asks.

We settle on the camouflage station. I spend a few minutes chatting with an instructor, and then I practice painting my face to blend in with trees. Pita, meanwhile, is speaking with a different instructor.

Holding a clipboard, the instructor asks, "Any previous camouflage experience?"

"Ten years of cake decorating," Pita says proudly.

"So, no experience then." Without looking up from his clipboard, the instructor checks off a box. "Got it."

We move on to other stations. In the back of the room, I see the Rainmakers watching us, jotting down notes and munching on snacks. I try not to think about them and instead focus my attention on learning as much as I can at each station. After a brief stop at the stationery station, where I pick up some nice cards for Prin, Pita and I find ourselves in front of the kissing station.

Pita clears his throat. "Uh . . . so, Kantkiss . . . should we maybe, I don't know, check out this station? It could be pretty useful in the arena," he says.

I hardly listen to what he says. I'm distracted.

"Pita," I say, "I think we're being followed."

Upon hearing this, Pita grips his food bag extra tightly. I spin around to see what it is that's unnerving me. I'm right. Someone is following us.

About ten feet behind me is a small crib, rocking back and forth, right beside the diaper-changing station. Inside, wearing pink booties and wrapped in a puffy blanket, is a little baby. It's the girl tribute from District 11. I squint to get a better look. She can't be a day over six months old.

"Pita," I say, dumbfounded, "look at that tribute. Look how little she is!"

The two of us slowly walk toward the crib. As we approach, she coos and spits up a bit. Pita starts making funny faces at her.

"Hey, check this out," Pita says, pointing to the side of

the crib. There, in flowery pink writing, are the words *Run Babyrun*. Pita slides his hand over it. "That must be her name. Run. Boy, they sure do have weird names in other districts, eh, Kantkiss?"

I nod. Looking at Run, lying there in her crib, I start to feel a little more confident about my chances in the Hunger Games. Compared to Run, I'm a pretty worthy competitor. I can walk, feed myself, and support the weight of my own head. I glance at Pita. He can do those things too, although he often complains about how heavy his head is. No, Run won't pose much of a problem for me in the arena. It's the Varsities I worry about.

The head trainer blows her whistle to announce a lunch break. It comes at the perfect time: Pita has just hit the bottom of his food sack. The tributes file into an adjacent cafeteria. It's set up a lot like the cafeteria back at my school, the main difference being that this cafeteria has food in it.

After I get my food, I look around for a place to sit. From a table in the back, Pita waves wildly at me. "KANTKISS!" he screams. "KANTKISS NEVERCLEAN!" I pretend not to hear him as I look for a different table. There are some cool-looking girls to my left, but when I turn in their direction, they avert their eyes. The kids at the next table do the same. Meanwhile, Pita is still hollering. "WE'LL MAKE IT A DISTRICT TWELVE TABLE! COME ON!" Finally, I relent and put my tray down next to Pita.

As we sit there, eating another delicious meal, I notice an absolutely massive tribute searching for a table. He's well over six feet tall—maybe seven. His thighs are like tree trunks. I'd seen him earlier at the boulder-throwing station, heaving enormous boulders across the room with ease. It was very impressive. A few Rainmakers had clapped. But what catches my eye now is not his size, it's what he's carrying. Tucked underneath his right arm is Run. Unable to find an empty table, he settles for a stand-up meal. The boy slides a diaper bag off his left arm, removes a bottle, and starts feeding Run.

"That's the other District Eleven tribute," Pita says with a mouthful of food. "His name's Smash."

"I'm going to invite him to join us," I say, desperate to avoid another meal listening only to the sound of Pita gorging himself. I do my best to smile as I wave him over. He pulls up a seat at our table and slams down the diaper bag.

"Me Smash," he says with a crooked grin. "You stay away from baby."

"Nice to meet you," Pita says.

"Me train hard. Kill everyone," Smash says.

Before we hear more of Smash's musings, we're told that the individual training sessions are beginning. This is our chance to show off our skills to the Rainmakers. Afterward, we're given scores that indicate our chances of success in the arena. Scores range from 1, totally screwed, to 12, cold-blooded killer.

The Rainmakers call in the first tribute. It's Archie from District 1. He crushes a beer can on his forehead before going inside the gymnasium. I slouch down in my chair as I realize that I'm going to be waiting for a long time before it's my turn. Pita, sensing my frustration, puts his hand on mine and smiles sympathetically.

Is this friendship I'm starting to feel toward Pita? He doesn't fit my two criteria for male friends—must 1) be super attractive and 2) have a girl's name. But maybe I've been too harsh on Pita. He might be a good friend after all. And judging by the way he's raising and lowering his eyebrows and making kissy sounds with his lips at me, I can tell he wants to be my friend too.

After what feels like a lifetime of waiting, the Rainmakers call me for my individual session. I'm feeling confident. But when I step inside the gym, I realize the odds are against me. The Rainmakers have seen twenty-three performances before me. They look bored.

"No more fighting!" one calls out. "Let's see a dance!"

"Yeah!" the Rainmakers shout. "Dance! Dance! Dance! Dance!"

I stay focused and grab a bow. I've decided to showcase my best skill, archery. But the archery range they've set up for me is too simple, just some blue and red targets painted on live humans. I know what will impress them. I launch into a one-woman dramatic rendition of a hunter pursuing a deer, playing both parts, hunter and deer.

When I get to the best part—squealing and frothing on the floor in my death throes as a wounded deer—I notice they've stopped booing. Awestruck, no doubt. But then I see it's because the Rainmakers have just been served a roast pheasant. I'm furious. Here I am, my life on the line, being judged by people who don't appreciate good theater when it lies on the ground frothing right in front of them.

Enough is enough. Without even thinking, I shoot an arrow right at the apple in the pheasant's mouth. I miss pretty badly and the arrow enters the chest of a Rainmaker and pins him, dead, against the wall.

Silence. A few agonizing seconds pass. Then, something strange happens. One of the Rainmakers begins a slow clap. *Clap . . . Clap . . . Clap.* And the other Rainmakers join in. Soon, they're all standing and they're roaring with applause. A few of them even whistle. "Good show!" one of them cries.

"We *hated* that guy," says another.

"Shoot Ralph again!" shouts another. So I do.

I can still hear the Rainmakers' raucous applause in my ears as I step into the elevator to head upstairs. When the doors slide open on the twelfth floor, Pita, Buttitch, and Effu are waiting for me.

"They're about to announce the scores!" Buttitch exclaims.

"And there are cookies in the dining room!" Pita shrieks.

We gather around the television to see the results. First they show each tribute's picture, then a picture of the animal they most resemble, then their score. Buttitch is jumping up and down with excitement. He's got a lot riding on these scores. "Come on, baby, give Daddy a seven!" he yells.

The Varsities all score between eight and ten. From floors below, I can hear them high-fiving and chest-bumping.

Smash, not surprisingly, scores an eleven. But what comes next is truly shocking. Baby Run gets a twelve.

"How did that happen?" I ask, bewildered.

"She really floored the Rainmakers during her private session," Pita says. "She made the stinkiest poo. It literally knocked out half the judges."

Now Pita's picture is on the screen, followed by an animated picture of a sloth turning into a fatter sloth. Everyone in the room holds their breath, except Pita, who can't do anything nearly that strenuous. His score flashes on the screen: zero.

"*Woo hoo!*" Buttitch cries. "Got that one right." He slaps Pita on the back proudly.

Pita looks sad. "I don't understand," he says.

"What happened in there?" I ask.

"I did everything perfectly," he says. "I walked in, thanked the Rainmakers for their time, and delivered a very humble and sincere speech about how I hope to perform well in the Hunger Games." Effu, Buttitch, and I stare at him blankly.

Before I can spend any time feeling bad for Pita, my picture is on the television. After an image of a weird, gamey-looking badger, the number twelve flashes on the screen.

"Yes!" I shout. The old deer routine has still got it.

"Goddamnit! Do you realize how much money you just cost me?" Buttitch screams, slamming his fist onto the coffee table.

As I look at that number twelve onscreen, I can't help thinking of Carol watching the television at home in District 12. I really miss him. I miss his gorgeous hair and beautiful face. I feel my knees go weak as I think about him. The past few days, I haven't had much time to daydream about Carol. Instead, my thoughts have been filled by another boy—Pita.

In the back of my mind, I wonder who my heart will belong to in the end. Will it be Carol, with his perfect body and unparalleled hunting skills? Or Pita, with his giant head and flabby stomach? It's a tough call. I ponder this as I look across the room at Pita, who's trying to lick a bread crumb stuck to his chin to save his arms the effort of moving up to get it.

"Tomorrow, you'll prepare for your interviews," Buttitch announces, as he rises to go to bed. "Get a good night's rest."

Before he can leave the room, Pita gets up and whispers something in Buttitch's ear. Buttitch nods, then turns toward me.

"Pita wants you to know that, going forward, he'd like to train separately from you."

Whatever. That is the first thought that runs through my head. It is a little bit interesting that Pita doesn't want to train with me anymore. But not very interesting. Definitely not interesting enough to warrant a cliffhanger.

"Are ya all right, mon?" Effu asks me, affectionately hovering her hand above my shoulder.

"Absolutely fine," I reply. This news has only changed my day a tiny amount.

"All right then," Effu says. "Let's go to ya room for ya trainin' session. *Without Pita.*"

Shrugging, I follow her. Effu is going to prepare me for my interview tonight, which will be televised and watched by everyone in Peaceland—sponsors included.

When we step into my room, Effu shrieks and quickly walks outside again. "I'm sorry, but this room smells like a poor person," she says. We waste an hour of precious training time waiting for a crew of Notalkses to fumigate it.

"Ah." Effu smiles as she reenters the room. "Much betta." I roll my eyes. Even though she can be a handful sometimes, I like Effu. We spend the next few hours going through my interview technique. Apparently I do not know how to smile. Effu tries to teach me how to move the muscles in my face so that the ends of my lips extend upward, but it feels very strange to me and eventually she gives up.

"At the very least ya have ta stop curling ya hand up into a fist and shakin' it at da person ya talking to, Kantkiss," she says with a sigh. We work on that for an hour with no results. Not only am I still shaking my fist, I have also started angrily kicking my leg.

"Well, I've done all I can do for ya," Effu concludes dejectedly when our time is up.

"Thank you for trying," I reply with a little kick, and head downstairs to find Buttitch. He tells me to change into a full-length gown and high-heel shoes. When I emerge from the dressing room, I am surprised to see he has done the same. I burst out laughing.

"Yeah, yeah. Very funny," he snarls. "Do you want to learn how to make an entrance or not?"

He spends the next couple of hours instructing me on walking. The shoes are the hardest part. The only other time I've ever worn high heels was on an incredibly ill-conceived hunting trip with Carol, and now I can barely walk to the other side of the room without falling down. Buttitch moves like he was born in heels, twirling gracefully and giving me the occasional curtsy just to show he isn't trying too hard.

If Buttitch can do it, so can I. After a while I get the hang of things, and Buttitch and I walk nimbly up and down the hallway together.

"Good," he grunts. "Now let's see how well you interview."

Buttitch takes the role of the interviewer and I answer his questions as best I can. Things are going pretty well. I've stopped kicking him and have even reduced the fist shaking to a passable wave. If I can keep this up, I figure I have a real shot of impressing the sponsors. But Buttitch isn't satisfied.

"No, no, no!" He stops me. "You need to be sexy! Here. Like this."

He flutters his eyelids, plays with the fabric of his dress flirtatiously, and giggles like a schoolgirl. I try to follow his example, but it's hopeless. I will never be sexy like Buttitch.

Buttitch spends the next half hour teaching me the secrets of seduction. Then, after glancing at his pager, he says, "When you get interviewed, make sure you cough exactly six times," he says. "No more, no less. Six. If you cough exactly six times, I think you have a good shot of winning over the sponsors."

It doesn't sound like a very good plan, but it's the only one I've got. I eat alone in my room that night. I'm so frustrated from training that I smash my plates against the wall, pretending that it is Buttitch doing one of his stupid curtsies. When Circle comes in to clean the mess, I shout, "Leave it alone!" and dive onto my bed, crying my eyes out.

I just want to be left alone. I hear a door close behind me. At first I think Circle has left my quarters, but then I realize she has gone into the bathroom. She returns with a damp washcloth and sits down on the bed next to me, stroking my hair soothingly. *I know Circle cares about me and isn't mad.* I calm down to let her wash the tears off my face, but then I recoil in pain. The washcloth is soaked in vinegar, and it stings my eyes very badly! I can't open my eyes, so eventually I just fall asleep.

The next morning my prep team wakes me up and instructs me to get naked. I groggily do as they say. As soon as I'm naked, they tell me to put on my clothes again, then they leave.

Cinnabon comes into the room. He is my last hope, a fashion genius.

"Hello, Kantkiss," Cinnabon says. "How are you doing today?"

Cinnabon is very kind, but I am too nervous for small talk. "I hope this dress is as beautiful as the last one, Cinnabon. It really needs to be," I say.

Cinnabon freezes and goes pale. "Dress!" he mouths. "Uh . . . I mean, yes. It is. Very beautiful. Close your eyes."

I do as he says and wait for what seems an eternity. I hear the sound of Cinnabon rummaging around the room, then the sound of him walking outside. Finally I hear his footsteps as he reenters the room. With my eyes still closed, Cinnabon fits me into his newest creation. After a few moments, he tells me to open my eyes.

I gasp as I see the creature standing before me in the full-length mirror. White strands of toilet paper twirl all around me, covering every inch of my body except for two eye slits. I am a mummy.

"Cinnabon!" I exclaim. "It's gorgeous! So scary!"

Cinnabon smiles. "Here's the best part." He pulls a cooking pot from behind his back and places it on my head. "There."

I can scarcely contain my excitement as I look in the mirror. I am not just a mummy but a warrior mummy. The cooking pot is my helmet. "Oh, Cinnabon," I manage at last, "*thank* you!"

"You are going to do fine in your interview," Cinnabon tells me. "Remember, just be yourself."

Just be myself? It's not a foolproof plan, but it's certainly better than what Buttitch came up with. "I'll try," I promise Cinnabon.

Then it's time to leave. The interview is filmed in front of a live studio audience. The other tributes and I file onto the stage and take our seats on a long couch. Jaesar Lenoman, the host of the interviews for the past twenty years, joins us in front of the cameras. He is a frightening man. His hair is a freakish mixture of bleached white and dyed gray. In the Capital they do surgery to make people look like monsters, and Jaesar Lenoman has paid a small fortune to extend his chin so that it nearly reaches his shirt. I can't imagine why anyone in the Capital would want to see a face like that on television, but somehow he is a huge success here.

"Thank you, thank you very much," Jaesar begins his monologue. "You might as well get comfortable, because you're not going anywhere till Monday!"

The next six minutes are the worst of my life.

"I don't know much about the Hunger Games," Jaesar quips, patting his belly. "But I'm odds-on favorite to win the Eating Games!" As the audience mindlessly laughs, I look around the stage for a weapon. I have to put an end to this. For Prin. I think of her being forced to watch this monologue at home and feel sick to my stomach. But there are no weapons on stage. I just have to sit there and bear it.

"Sometimes my wife wishes I was a Notalks," Jaesar continues. "That way I couldn't tell her what I think of her cooking!" He pretends to be a Notalks, making gestures with his hands to show he is choking on his wife's food. If Carol were here, he'd know what to do. He would shoot me through the heart with an arrow to put me out of my misery. But Carol isn't here. I shudder to think what he must be going through, how he also has to watch this monologue.

I am on the verge of passing out from the monologue when Jaesar stops for a commercial break. When we go back on air, the interviews begin. It takes me a while to recover from the jokes, and when I look up, Jaesar is already interviewing the boy tribute from District 3, the moral qualms district. A thoughtful, bookish boy who chooses his words carefully, he is pinning all his hopes on his recollection of Sun Tzu's *The Art of War*, although he admits he has difficulty overlooking the ethical tensions in the work. Tributes from the moral qualms district always do very badly in the Hunger Games.

I sit like a lady, the way Buttitch showed me, as the districts slip by. The tributes all interview well, and it makes me nervous. Gatsby Rockefeller CCXLIV, the boy tribute from District 6—the old money district—is perfectly at ease in front of the cameras. He disdainfully tells Jaesar that the Games are no different than a good fox hunt and that his father will hear if anything happens to him. When Jaesar tells him that his three minutes are up, Gatsby threatens to have him fired.

Out of the corner of my eye, I see Effu waving in my direction, desperately trying to tell me something. "I wish that Gatsby was my tribute instead of you!" she whispers when I look up. I roll my eyes.

Even Run, the baby from District 11, gives an impressive interview. She spends the first two minutes giggling and pointing at the stage lights, which is very cute, then blows everyone away by saying her first word, *ketchup*, on live television. The audience gives her a standing ovation as she crawls back to her seat. If only I were a baby. I could get away with the giggling and first-word strategy. I bet most of the sponsors are at least considering her right now.

Smash, the towering tribute from District 11, takes a different approach. "Training *good*," he grunts, then picks up Jaesar and lifts him high above his head. Before anyone can explain to him that the private training sessions are over, Smash throws Jaesar into the audience and returns to his seat.

Then it's my turn to be interviewed. Jaesar brushes some dirt off his suit and says, "I haven't taken a fall like that since last season's ratings came in!" As the audience hoots and applauds, I again feel nauseous. I will be sitting less than three feet away from Jaesar during our interview. It will be impossible to ignore his jokes.

"So, Kantkiss," Jaesar says, getting down to business, "What do you think of the Capital?"

My mind goes blank. Desperately, I seek out Cinnabon in the audience. "Just be honest," he mouths encouragingly, giving me two thumbs-up.

"Well," I begin, "obviously I hate the Capital. All of my life it has oppressed me and my family, making us live in poverty and killing my dad, and now it is forcing me to fight to the death against kids. I just completely hate it."

The words come out before I can stop them. I gulp. I've definitely gone too far this time. Cinnabon's advice sounded so reasonable!

Jaesar and the rest of the audience look at me quizzically. Any second now I will be taken to the Capital's prisons and tortured for inciting revolution. Maybe they will turn me into a Notalks instead of killing me. I just pray they don't hurt my family.

But when Jaesar finally speaks, he sounds amused rather than angry. "What was that, mummy? I couldn't hear a word you said through that scary costume of yours!" I breathe a huge sigh of relief. Cinnabon to the rescue again.

"That reminds me of the time I flew Egyptian Airways," Jaesar continues. "Do you want to hear about that?"

Vigorously, I shake my head and make my scariest warrior mummy sounds. But it's no use. The audience shouts and encourages Jaesar to tell his story and he does, complete with airplane food jokes and a whole routine about how he has to take off his shoes at airport security but is then told to put them back on because his feet are so smelly. While sitting through his act, I silently renew my vow never to have children. Only a monster would bring life into a world where these kinds of jokes are told.

The only good thing about Jaesar's story is that it takes up all the remaining interview time. As I return to my seat, I see Buttitch tearing up a betting slip and cursing furiously. I forgot to cough six times.

Next up is Pita. He wins over the audience from the start by asking everyone in the front row how their days are going and making small talk with them. Finally, Jaesar gets him to sit down in the interview chair. Jaesar has a hard time interviewing Pita because Pita has so many questions of his own. He is genuinely interested in Jaesar's life, pleasantly inquiring about his family, health, and hobbies.

"So tell me," Jaesar manages after answering several of Pita's questions about his hovercraft collection, "did you leave a girlfriend behind in District Twelve?"

Pita sighs. "Well, there is one girl."

The audience hoots and asks for more information. Some people in the audience even blow Pita kisses. It is a very unusual audience.

"I have a girlfriend," Pita continues, "but I'm getting tired of that broad. I feel like she's cramping my style, you know?" He looks directly in the camera. "Emily, if you are watching this, it's over. I am breaking up with you."

"Ah . . . that's too bad," Jaesar says. "So there's no special lady in your life anymore?"

"Actually, there is," Pita says. "Her." I gasp when I realize he is pointing at me.

I am absolutely furious. What right does Pita—or any boy for that matter—have to say that he *likes* me? I have never been this irrationally angry! It is one thing to pretend in training that we are friends. But to say that he *likes* me? That I am *special*? On *television*? That crosses the arbitrary line that exists in my head, and I won't stand for it!

Outraged, I rise from my seat and march over to Pita. When he turns, I punch him in the face as hard as I can, knocking him off the stage.

"Ouch! Wouldn't you like to learn the story behind that punch?" Jaesar asks the audience, as Pita totters groggily back to the stage. "Unfortunately, rules are rules, and this show is scheduled to end now. Stay tuned for an all-new episode of *President Bernette Is a Wise and Just Leader,* coming up next!"

I am still fuming when I get back to my quarters. The rest of my team is there, and they are furious at me.

"What the hell were you thinking back there?" Buttitch shouts. "You didn't cough once!"

"Uh . . . more to da point," Effu interjects, "why did ya punch Pita?"

"Because he said he liked me," I explain patiently, "in front of *people.*" Duh. *Why doesn't anybody understand where I'm coming from?*

"He made ya desirable!" Effu retorts. "Now dat Pita has

said he likes you, everybody else will too. Dat's how relation-ships work, Kantkiss!"

I am starting to waver. Maybe my team has a point. Maybe I was too harsh with Pita when I punched him in the face as hard as I could.

Just then Pita stumbles into the room, crying. "You . . . you hit me so *hard*," he manages between tears.

"I'm sorry, Pita," I say. "I shouldn't have punched you."

Pita cheers up when he hears my apology. "Even though my face still stings," he says, "my feelings don't hurt anymore. And feelings are what matter."

We watch the replay of the interviews over dinner, and my team assures me that my punching gaffe didn't ruin the starstruck lovers angle. "I thought you were putting a scary mummy love curse on him," says Cinnabon.

Then it is time to say good-bye to Buttitch and Effu. There won't be time tomorrow. Effu wishes me good luck in the arena but refuses to shake my hand. "What if one of my high society friends is watching troo da window?" she says.

"Any final advice?" I ask Buttitch.

"Stay alive," he grunts. Then he leans into my ear and whispers, "And kill Pita on the fourth day with a blunt instru-ment. You put me in a real hole with that coughing busi-ness."

I promise him I'll think about it. On my way to my room, I see Pita staring out the window. He looks over the Capital's skyline, lost in thought.

"What's on your mind?" I ask him.

"I just hope . . ." he begins emotionally, "I just hope that all of the tributes will stay friends after the Hunger Games end!"

Groaning, I walk to my bedroom and fall asleep. It's not easy. I'm pretty nervous about tomorrow, the start of the Games.

Cinnabon wakes me up the next morning and takes me to the roof, where a hovercraft is waiting for us. A Pacemaker tells me to be still and sticks a needle in my forehead.

"Ouch!" I exclaim.

"Shhh . . . That's just your tracker," Cinnabon reassures me, "so that the Capital will know where you are at all times."

"But they take it out after the Hunger Games end, right?" I ask. "Say that I returned to the Capital as part of a secret revolution . . . hypothetically speaking, of course. Would they be able to track me?"

"Of course not!" the Pacemaker says, aghast. "The Capital takes your personal privacy very seriously in this one particular case! You have rights, you know." I breathe a sigh of relief.

As Cinnabon and I board the hovercraft, a Pacemaker walks by with a large cowbell. "We ran out of trackers," he explains. "One tribute will have to make do with this."

The hovercraft journey is short. Before I know it, we land and I am ushered to my platform in the launch room. Any minute now I will enter the arena and the Games will begin.

"I almost forgot to give you this," Cinnabon says, taking

out my THE CAPITAL SUCKS! pin and fastening it on my outfit. "It barely cleared inspections because of how sharp it is. You're lucky. The inspectors declared one tribute's token a weapon, and he was disqualified on the spot."

I gulp. "What happened to him?"

Cinnabon shakes his head sadly. "He was immediately sent home. He will never have the honor of competing in the Hunger Games."

Just then a voice booms over the arena's loudspeakers, "Errwl halwannn hoanwah wohhhhh!"

"Bear with us, folks," another announcer's voice follows. "Greg, our announcer, is a Notalks from our Jobs for Felons program. He was trying to say, 'Ladies and Gentlemen, welcome to the Hunger Games!'"

My tube rises into the arena. The golden Cornucrapia lies straight ahead, its mouth brimming with weapons and supplies. The Varsities will no doubt call first pick on the Hula-Hoops. I can survive by exercising my core with old-fashioned Pilates, but I seethe with jealousy to think of them toning so easily. The inexperienced tributes will go straight for the stacks of old *TV Guides*, which look great but you can find all that information online nowadays. Buttitch would want me to run for the forest immediately, but that's just because he fears strong independent women. I refuse to let gender roles decide whether or not I am bludgeoned to death with a pogo stick.

Before we begin, I take a look at my surroundings. All things considered, I lucked out on location. There's a lake for water, a forest for cover, and a synagogue for prayer.

During the training period, I overheard horror stories about the Forty-Fourth Hunger Games. They say it took place in an Arby's. Those who weren't killed by the other tributes willingly starved to death. Other years were no better. An abandoned coal mine, a nonabandoned hippie commune, inside a whale: I could be a lot worse off.

The voice of Greg the Announcer booms over the intercom. "Leh ah sebity fawb Ugga Gaes bega!"

For a moment, all is silent. "Um, what?" asks a visibly confused Pita.

"Ah se, leh ah Gaes bega!" repeats Greg.

A few of the tributes look at each other and shrug. Suddenly a brighter, clearer voice comes over the intercom. "Hey, great job there, Greg. This is Greg's supervisor again, and just to reiterate, 'Let the Seventy-Fourth Hunger Games begin!'"

The intercom clicks off, and I begin counting down the sixty seconds until I can move. Until then, we're bound to our starting discs by a strict honor code (the television broadcast is at a commercial break).

I stare at the Cornucrapia and weigh my options. The Blu-ray player thirty yards in will be useful if I find any *Will & Grace* box sets, but a pristine pair of Hulk Hands lies twenty yards to its right. About ten yards off I spy a pot lid, glimmering in the sunlight. People tell stories in the Crack about a boy winning the Hunger Games with just a pot lid, although back then they took place in Japan and were referred to as *Battle Royale*.

Past the Cornucrapia, I spot an ugly tribute from District 5, who looks a lot like a dog. I cleverly decide to nickname her Dogface. Right now she's staring into space absentmind-edly, picking her nose.

My best plan looks like taking the Ouija board right in the Cornucrapia. Ghosts make powerful allies. I'm all set to go for it when I see Pita waving to get my attention. "Kantkiss," he yells, "don't go for the Cornucrapia. Go to the woods. For God's sake, please go to the woods. Going to the Cornucrapia is something an idiot would do." *What does he mean? Does he want me to go to the Cornucrapia or not?*

I'm still trying to figure him out when the cannon goes off, and the other tributes leave me in the dust. *Stupid Pita! Why did you rush me at the listening comprehension station?*

It's too late to snag the goods in the Cornucrapia. Gatsby has taken all the Dijon mustard, and Dogface is eating the baseball I was eyeing. There are still plenty of roast turkeys left, but after all the braised peacock I ate in the Capital, I'm not ready to go back to peasant food just yet. Everything else is being snatched up right in front of me. The tree I could hide in? Smash is hugging it. The bathroom scale I could throw? A fat tribute is standing on it. The automatic rifle I could shoot? It's right next to me, but I'm afraid I'll appear desperate.

Not wanting to leave empty-handed, I grab a black back-pack five feet in front of me. I know this backpack will stick out like a sore thumb against any pumpkin patches or traffic cone sculptures I run into, so I grab a can of orange paint for camouflage. I'm about to make a break for the woods when I feel something tug at my pack. It's one of the other tributes! I knew I should have painted the bag immediately.

"Give me that!" he shouts. He's about to pull it clear off my back when he goes stiff, like a cow the second before you punch it.

"What's wrong?" I ask. He just stands there, blindly clutching for his own back. "Suddenly my backpack isn't good enough for you?" I rail on. He stumbles sideways and starts coughing blood like a holier-than-thou jerk, mocking my equipment in what must be the traditional mockery dance of his district. He's trying to psych me out, make me feel inadequate about my gear. He finally falls over and I see the knife sticking out of his back. I guess I wouldn't want a backpack either if I had a knife.

I look up and see a girl staring at me about twenty feet off, wearing a belt filled with knives. *How does everyone have a knife but me?* I think maybe I can barter one for some of my paint, but before I even ask her, she helpfully tosses one at my head. It misses and flies off into the woods. I toss her the grenade lying next to me as thanks, though I keep the pin for my collection. I smile as I skip over to the tree the knife is lodged in. From behind me I hear her scream, *"Nooo—!"* but I really don't mind walking over to get the knife. I'm glad to have a new friend. I turn around to thank her, but all that's left is a leg and a blood smear. *Hm . . . I wonder where she went. These games can be so unpredictable.*

I know I should escape into the woods, but I decide to take one last look at the battlefield the Cornucrapia has become. The bodies of fallen tributes haven't been collected yet. The Rainmakers usually wait until the initial bloodbath dies down so that tributes can still trip hilariously over the corpses.

Only a few living tributes have stuck around the battle-field. The theater district tributes are using bodies to re-create a tableau from *Les Mis,* and the boy from the moral qualms district is debating whether he should help the one tribute he has an 80 percent chance of saving or the four tributes he has a 20 percent chance of saving. I don't see Pita anywhere, but that means he's still alive, or at least died in a cool enough way not to leave a body.

When I turn to leave, a sound blares over the intercom. *BWOMMP BWOMMP.* It's the sad trombone used to announce the deaths of the tributes. *BWOMMP BWOMMP. BWOMMP BWOMMP. BWOMMP BWOMMP.*

I count eleven sad trombones before they finally stop. If there's one trombone for each dead tribute, and there were twenty-four tributes when we started, and twenty-four hours in a day, and the Games have been going on for less than an hour, and there are sixty minutes in an hour, and it's taken me two hours to get this far in my equation, then there must be at least forty tributes left! Competition is heating up fast.

As I hike into the woods, it becomes clear that I need to find something to drink. My backpack only contained saltines and a slab of pound cake, which I ate immediately to lighten the load. I think back to the gourmet root beer and artisanal sodas I had in the Capital and nearly collapse into the river I'm walking in. *Buttitch, why won't you send me something? Is it because you hate me? Or . . . or is it because*

you know I'm right near something I can use? Oh my God! The river! I can use water from the river to make single-batch root beer!

I set up a camp next to the river and start constructing a rudimentary still out of rocks and twigs. Now that I have water, all I have to do is find sassafras, cloves, honey, cinnamon, vanilla, cherry tree bark, and the other twenty-four flavors. My artisanal root beer is so close I can almost taste it, but the sun is setting and I need my rest. I'll have to sleep first. I camouflage my still with some leaves and climb up into a tall tree to sleep. When I'm about thirty feet up, I loop my belt around the branch and then around my neck, so if I fall out, I won't live to experience the shame.

Just as I'm about to nod off, the Peaceland emblem lights up the sky and smooth jazz pipes over the intercom. Of course! How could I forget the evening announcements? Each night, the Capital informs the tributes about who died that day and other pertinent information.

The smooth jazz gets softer as a sonorous DJ chimes in. "Hey there, this is your old pal Rusty Jams, and you cats are in the Hunger Games. This song is going out to my main man Archie, who's taking it easy with a couple of his closest friends and a beautiful lakeside view. Damn, Archie. You know how to live it good."

I bite my lip with nervousness at the thought of finding out who died. What if something happened to Pita? What if I died but don't realize I'm a ghost? I whack my head a few times to make sure it's solid as the saxophones play on.

"That last one was for my girl Sarah from District Nine, who's already catching some Zs, and who can blame her? She sure does look sweet tucked away in that mulberry bush near the distinctly triangular rock by the lake. She doesn't even seem worried that the Varsities have set up camp only thirty feet from her, much less that she's directly visible from where they are standing. That girl's tough as nails."

Another smooth jazz song plays for about twenty seconds before it's interrupted by the BWOMMP BWOMMP of a sad trombone. An audibly startled Rusty Jams comes back on the intercom. "That uh, was in memory of my girl Sarah, who uh, really knew how to live. No more smooth jazz tonight."

His microphone cuts off, and they start projecting the images of the fallen tributes. First up is a boy I don't recognize, then the girl with the knives. More tributes are shown before a little placard saying In Memoriam flashes across the sky and a thoughtful Yo-Yo Ma cello piece begins playing. After the initial tribute announcements, Peaceland honors film and television celebrities who died during the year.

First up is Tom Piper, host of the hit series *Notalkses Say the Darndest Things*. Next is Oscar Powell, the legend who directed *Dude, Where's My Hovercraft?* From a distance, I hear the unmistakable sobbing of the theater district tributes.

I wake up a little before dawn. It's not quite light out, but something is going on below me. I shift on my branch to take a look around, but there's no one in sight. Then I hear it: *DONG! DONG! DONG!* It's the tribute with the bell around his neck. I had thought the Rainmakers would slip him a subdermal tracker when they got another shipment, but I guess those things are pretty expensive. The tribute runs out of some bushes and makes a panicked beeline for my tree, grunting and straining against the heavy weight of the cast-iron bell strapped around his neck.

That's when I see the Varsities behind him. I can only make out Archie's outline in the darkness, but I know there must be four or five of them. In one fluid motion, Archie winds up and throws something at the bell tribute. It spirals perfectly through the air before connecting with the tribute's head. As I watch in horror, the bell rolls into a patch of moonlight, followed by the bloody steel football that Archie threw, and then finally the tribute's severed head. "Bro," one of the Varsities says to Archie, "sick."

BWOMMP BWOMMP. I can hardly believe what I'm seeing. Archie has taken the great game of football and made it a vehicle for violence. The other Varsities all chest-bump with Archie. "Bro, that was so tight," one says.

"Archie, you're so strong!" fawns Mandy, who can somehow check her clothes, boobs, and makeup in one fluid motion.

"Let's get out of here, guys," says one of the pack, but there's something about that voice that throws me off. The husky tone, the rhythmic clapping of chins, the gentle hints of dough and French bread . . . Pita!

"Look, breadboy, this isn't just about killing people," shoots back Archie. "It's about going out and giving one hundred ten percent, never saying never, and not throwing in the towel when the chips are down. Other people will never have the opportunity to smell a severed head or hear the sound a rib makes when you hit someone in the brain with it. Stop being so afraid of new experiences, sissy."

One of the taller Varsities slaps Pita in the boobs and adds, "Yeah, you're as bad as your *girlfriend*."

With that, Archie picks up his football and says, "All right, let's find another loser." They do a quick huddle to get amped up and then chug some Muscle Milk.

They're gone as soon as they appeared, leaving me with more questions than answers. *Pita, what were you doing with those guys? Are you really playing this thing to win?*

I want to be worried, but smelling Pita has made me so hungry, it's hard to think of anything else. As I wait to make sure they're gone, I watch as a hovercraft appears in the sky above the body. Each time a tribute dies, a hovercraft shows up to remove the body. As it descends, the craft's door slides open. Two voices are faintly audible from inside.

"So I probably won't open the restaurant until Becky's out of school."

"That's fair. She needs a dad, not a manager."

"Of course Jennifer wants me to stick with this hovercraft thing awhile longer. Says it's reliable money."

"Well, what's reliable about it the other eleven months of the year?"

"Tell me about it. This guy got a head anywhere?"

"Oh yeah, by the stream."

"Great, got it. Hey, you know any good trout recip—"

The doors slam shut and the hovercraft floats off. Now that it's finally safe, I undo my belt and fall thirty feet out of the tree to the ground below. When I come to, it's midafternoon, and I'm even hungrier than before. I barely manage to choke out a message to Buttitch: "Please, send designer sushi . . . root beer . . ." I've given up on trying to make my own food or trying to climb ten feet to the gift of roast quail and sparkling cider that has gotten caught on a branch above me in a parachute.

It's time to throw myself on the mercy of the sponsors. "Please," I beg to whoever is watching me, "please don't let me die like this. I could die so much more violently." A few moments pass, and I'm delighted to see a package fall right next to me. Swordfish and pomegranate spritzer! And a flamethrower. These sponsors are sharp.

The food is delicious. By the time I'm finished, I feel great. I start preparing to find some better supplies. But oh no! I left my backpack all the way up in the branch where I slept. "Please," I plead tearfully, "please get me another backpack. That one is way up there and I'm so tired of climbing." Nothing happens. "*Sooooooo* tired."

A package falls out of the sky and hits me painfully on the head. It's a rock with a message written on it. I pick it up. It says "Screw You, Kantkiss." Sponsors can pay extra to comically whack tributes with their gifts. One year the games were won this way by a boy whose sponsor sent every other tribute a bowling ball to the head. At least I can throw the rock up at my backpack, I think. I give the rock a mighty toss and it knocks the backpack loose, exactly as planned. Then it falls to the ground and hits the flamethrower, which is a happy accident until the flamethrower goes off, making it a regular accident.

I grab my backpack. The flamethrower is going crazy, whipping around and setting all the trees on fire. I hop over logs, branches, and the occasional camera crew with the flames licking at my back. I feel bad for the dead cameramen, but they died getting great footage. "Run!" I call out to anyone who can hear me. "The Rainmakers have started a forest fire!"

The fire is blazing and its heat starts to burn my cheeks. The flames are closing in on me. I need a way to escape. I consider my options. *If I run through the fire, like really fast, can it burn me?* As I step backward to start my sprint through the roaring wall of flames, I bump into the trunk of a large tree. I decide to climb high above the flames, since only its lower branches are on fire.

I make it to the top of the tree. *Not bad, Kantkiss.* My eyes and lungs are filled with smoke, but I manage to wink at a cameraman in a parallel branch and announce, "I'm all *fired* up!" I hope Prin is watching at home, adding this latest quip to the list I imagine she keeps. I repeat this catchphrase sporadically until the fire dies out an hour later.

The end of the fire is not the end of the danger below. Beneath me I hear the cracking twigs and high fives of the Varsities. From the way they're saying, "I see her in that tree," I know they're moments from discovering me. I try counting the Varsities but stop once I realize I'm outnumbered. Suddenly, the scent of freshly baked bread comes wafting through the air. *Pita is with them!* I try to make eye contact, but he avoids my gaze, so I alternate between glaring at the top of his fat head and trying to raise one eyebrow at the camera.

Meanwhile, Archie Nemesis, the Varsities' captain, has gotten out a small whiteboard and gathered his team into a huddle. He scribbles furiously on the board, barking commands. I gasp when I see what he has drawn. It's a single arrow — an arrow pointing right at me. *Masterful play design.*

Archie begins to climb the tree. What an idiot! His muscles are way too big and heavy to make it up this weeping willow. *SNAP.* I'm hoping he's dead from the fall, but when I look down, I see he's still clinging to the tree. *CRACKLE . . . POP!* Down below, Pita has begun eating a bowl of Rice Krispies.

SHAZAM. Finally, the sound I've been waiting for. The branch gives, and Archie falls back to where he came from.

"Here, take this, Archie," says a well-dressed Varsity from District 7, offering his captain a silver chain saw. He must have picked it up at the Cornucrapia.

"What? Do you want me to cut off your head or something?" says Archie, pushing away the saw. "Here's what you need to understand: I am very angry right now!"

I see the oblong, steel football clutched in his beefy hand. *THUD.* The whole tree shakes as he hurls it into the trunk. *Sports really are a great way to relieve stress!* Another Varsity picks up the ball and jogs it back to Archie. *THUD.*

If they keep this up, I'll never be able to sleep. *They won't be able to sleep either*, I comfort myself as I drift off.

It is evening when I wake up to the sound of rustling in a neighboring tree. Here in the arena, a sound could mean anything. For example, if the sound comes from a person, it could be words, and those words, again, could mean anything. I decide to investigate. I turn my head slowly and find myself facing a raccoon with a baby bottle in its paw. The raccoon is not alone: it's nursing a tribute.

Run, the baby tribute from District 11.

How long has she been there? And how long has she had an alliance with that raccoon? The whole time probably. The raccoon burps her, slides a pacifier into her mouth, and bops her on the nose. I never would have thought to form an alliance with anything but a human. Run could have sent her raccoon hit man to kill me while I slept. Unless she has some ulterior motive, I don't understand why she didn't. I wish I could get inside her cute squishy head.

I reluctantly turn my attention back to the raccoon, which twitches its whiskers and silently points its paw at the tree above me.

I look up and see something hanging on a branch fifteen feet up. It takes me a minute to make out what it is, but after exactly sixty seconds, I get it. It's a wasp nest, but the surface is so crazy, like it's breathing. *Whoa*. It's totally intense and beautiful. I know what made this: LSBees.

Long stinger bees are a type of transformation, or as we in the districts call them, *trannies*. Trannies are artificial species genetically engineered by the Capital for use as weapons against the people. Years ago, LSBees were designed for the purpose of government mind control. Soon after their release into the districts, they proved to be too dangerous and unpredictable for official use. Just one LSBee sting will make you hallucinate. Too many can kill you. I've never encountered LSBees in the wild before, but I know I have to be careful. Bugs are so scary!

At this point, I start to feel lonely. I'm in a tree surrounded by alliances. The Varsities are below me, Run and the raccoon are beside me, and the LSBees are above in their cliquey hive. Suddenly, I'm angry. This game isn't about which tribute is the strongest or smartest or fastest. It's a stupid popularity contest, just like school. Even doughy Pita left me. *If I can't have friends, no one should be able to.* Run and the raccoon have disappeared into the darkness, so I decide to break up the alliance closest to me: the LSBees.

I need to act quickly and quietly. I'll cut the nest while everyone is sedated by the silky smooth tones of the evening jazz. If all goes well, the Varsities will die painful deaths from the LSBee attack and I'll be binge-eating away my sorrows with delicious honey.

When the emblem flashes and the DJ comes on, I shimmy toward the nest and pull a fork and knife out of my backpack. I balance tenuously on the branch, stabilizing it with my fork and cutting it with the knife. *You can't lose focus for a minute in these games*, I think, drifting off to sleep.

I wake up in the morning to the sound of the Varsities

laughing and slapping each other's butts. They think they're so cool, but none of the other tributes *really* like them. I comfort myself with the thought that their home life is probably plush but unfulfilling.

I get back to work cutting down the nest. It doesn't take long.

SHAZAMALAM. The branch snaps and the LSBee nest tumbles down with it.

It lands right on top of the Varsities. They shake their fists at me, then start panicking and swatting at the insects. "I wouldn't want to *bee* them!" I announce to the viewers back home, flashing my trademark grin.

I feel a pinch on my hand. "Ouch!" I scream. One of the LSBees has popped out of the nest and stung me. *Oh no.* I begin to worry that my plan has backfired when I hear a buzzing in my ears and feel a prick on my neck. Suddenly I'm filled with an overwhelming sense of peace. *Ah, that's better.* I know I shouldn't get stung by LSBees, but it feels so good.

The sun gets brighter, the flowers more flowery. When I look down at the Varsities, I no longer see murderers. I see friends. Then a little while later I see giant chipmunks playing catch with a giant acorn.

I feel the insatiable desire to hug each and every one of them. I begin by hugging the tree for practice as I descend to the forest floor. When I hit the ground tail first, I realize that I too am a chipmunk. *How did I never realize that I was a chipmunk before?*

My furry fellows are scurrying about, swatting LSBees

with their tails and talking their high-pitched chipmunk talk. I do not understand the language yet, but I am eager to learn more about my chipmunk heritage. I casually lean against a pinecone while surveying my surroundings.

I notice one chipmunk slumped over in the middle of the clearing. I instinctively look both ways before getting closer. When I safely bridge the gap, my worst fear is realized: road kill. What car did this? And why did my friend have to go so soon? I let out a long squeal of anguish.

I reach down to stroke his shoulder with my tail, but I can't feel anything. I gasp as my tail vanishes into thin air. Everything begins to swirl out of focus around me, until I realize that it was all a hallucination. When I regain my sight, I am standing over the dead body of the male tribute from District 7.

I hear footsteps coming toward me. I run and duck behind a bush for cover, surprising a real family of chipmunks and feeling a bit jealous. I take another step and realize that something is caught on my ankle. It's a bow and arrow!

"Good find," I say, congratulating my ankle.

"Anytime, Kantkiss," my ankle replies. *Maybe this LSBee venom hasn't completely worn off yet.*

I load an arrow in the bow and shoot right into the middle of the ground so the cameras can see how good I am. I'm about to shoot an apple off my own head with a tricky backward shot when I see something out of the corner of my eye. It's Archie scribbling furiously on his whiteboard with a murderous grin on his face.

I know absolutely nothing about football, but whatever Archie is planning looks like a pyramid play, a three-man defensive play banned by the NCAA upon the conclusion of the 1933 season. Whatever it is, it's certainly designed to kill me. He's about to draw one last line when we both look up, smelling a familiar doughy scent.

Pita—that traitor—comes charging into view. Great. *Now this will be a two-on-one kill*, I think. At least it will happen faster this way. I begin to ready myself for death by changing into a pair of clean underpants that a sponsor sends, but then something amazing happens. Pita violently jerks the dry-erase marker from Archie's hand, draws a huge X through the play, and tries to break the whiteboard in two. Unable to achieve this feat of strength, Pita resorts to sitting on the board so Archie cannot see any of the play.

Before I can run, Archie gets out his steel football. He drops back to pass, but accidentally slams into Pita. Archie lands hard on his head and lies motionless on the ground.

"Pita, I'm going to live!" I scream joyfully. *Silence.* "Pita, aren't you going to say something?" *More silence.* "P-i-i-i-t-a-a-a-," I whine. I think something happened to Pita.

I approach his soft, curvy figure slumped over the whiteboard. His pointer finger is bleeding a little bit. "Oh Pita!" I cry, stooping to the ground and cradling his wounded finger. He wakes up to my touch.

"Kantkiss, I'll be okay," he says, promptly fainting again at the sight of his finger blood. His large head thuds down on my lap. It's so heavy that my legs immediately begin losing circulation. *Is this just another plot to kill me? Didn't he just save my life?* I'm not sure if Pita is a friend or an enemy or an enemy with benefits, but he definitely looks peaceful with his eyes closed. He even looks kind of cute.

Whoosh. I look up as the metallic football whizzes over my head. Archie's back on his feet, and his team is with him. They have us surrounded. They're playing a friendly game of catch to warm up before killing us.

"Pita, save me again!" I shriek, but by this point he's too far gone. Looks like this is it. I prepare to die in disgrace.

Suddenly the earth shakes and a very unusual creature comes galloping into the clearing.

"Oh no!" exclaims one of the Varsity tributes. "It's a shart!"

The shart is one of the Capital's most chilling trannies. Part great white shark, part Siberian tiger, the shart combines the most terrifying parts of land and sea. Sharts were originally created to be pets for young children in the Capital, but that went horribly, so they were exiled to the districts. I didn't know there were any sharts still alive today, but then again I don't read the news much.

"Let's get out of here, bra," Archie says to the rest of his team. They bounce, leaving me with the shart.

ROARGLUB! The shart turns on me, brandishing its rows of mismatched teeth and flopping its dorsal fin. It's too bad I am going to die now, but I have to admit this thing is awesome.

I begin reciting my last words to a terrified cameraman.

"Tell my mom she looks fat no matter what clothes she wears," I say. Just then I hear a big thump and see the shart has collapsed on the ground.

Glopglopglopgrowl... The shart frantically gasps for water, its gills completely dry. After a few moments it goes still, and a special shart trombone sounds to signify its death. Poor shart. I consider giving it a burial, but in the end I decide to just cremate it. After the ceremony I get really tired. "Later, Pita," I say, climbing up a nearby tree. *I would give anything for a hit of LSBee right now*, I think, as I doze off.

I awake in a haze. I am exhausted, dehydrated, and in grave danger (duh!).

A haze is another of the Capital's transformations, a tree designed to produce hazelnut-flavored coffee from a spout along its trunk. It is indistinguishable from a normal hazelnut tree except for its branches, which are huge pillows. I must have been caught in its snares while falling out of a very tall tree. I sit up and smell the Capital's bitter coffee.

I'm a few yards away when I hear a big noise. I remember a thing my father always said: "When you hear a big noise, remember my advice." *Oh man, then what did he say?*

I shrug and prepare for danger. I strike my best "hiding behind a tree" pose and arrange my face into my finest "scared and waiting for an unknown assailant" expression. I hope the cameras are getting this, because now I'm doing a very convincing "peaceful acceptance of death's imminence" face.

I hear the noise again. It is coming from the direction of the haze. I look into the branches and see an adorable baby curled up on a very fluffy pillow. Run is still alive! The noise I heard was her cute baby snoring.

Since she and the raccoon saved me from the LSBees, I feel myself wanting to protect Run. Right now, she's sleeping like an angel, but all I can envision is her death. Any second now a big noisy tribute is going to emerge from the haze to tear her limbs off and eat them one by one. Then he'll come for me with her blood still dripping from his jaws. When he eats me, our bloods will commingle in his stomach, and Run will become my blood sister, just like Prin. The thought fills me with peace.

"Run! Run!" I yell, inadvertently causing Dogface to reveal her hiding place in the middle of a treeless field and sprint screaming into the forest.

Run stretches her little arms upward to show that she is awake and unarmed. It seems like a symbolic gesture of peace, but I'm no fool.

"Prepare to die," I say, calmly raising my bow.

My arrow pierces the ripe young flesh of a nearby salamander. I must make offerings of food if I hope to gain Run's trust. I approach her cautiously. She could easily be concealing weapons inside that lumpy diaper of hers. Besides, she is strategically positioned on high ground. I cook the salamander using a lighter I found in the Cornucrapia. I hope the scent of delicious food will lure Run from her perch.

"Run, would you like to form an alliance with me?" I ask.

Run opens her mouth as if to begin speaking, but no words come out. She is left speechless by my magnanimous proposition.

"I know what you're thinking. Why would a high-scoring tribute like me, a seventeen-year-old—not quite a girl, not yet a woman, possibly a man—want to form an alliance with a helpless baby like yourself?"

Run nods her head in agreement in the uncoordinated way babies do when drifting off to sleep.

"Stop that, Run. Quit that attitude. It is a bad attitude. You are not just a helpless baby. You are a very clever baby. You are the best baby in these Games. Someday you too may blossom into a woman."

Run begins to giggle. She's tough to crack, but I can tell I am beginning to break through her icy veneer. On an unrelated note, in the tree behind me, a squirrel has just fallen out of a tiny hammock.

"Yes, that is a good point, Run, only one of us can survive the Hunger Games and become a woman. Why should you trust *me*? Well, let me reveal to you my deepest, darkest secret: I could never kill a baby! Babies like you remind me of myself, peeing and slobbering all over the place. You're just like me!"

Run rolls onto her stomach and skeptically buries her face in the pillow.

"Even if the Hunger Games come down to the two of us, I will not kill you. I can't, at least not until you reach the late stages of your toddler years. Think how much fun we could have. The arena would be our playground. You could live freely and play amongst the cuddly animals until I slaughter them for our food."

Run doesn't move or make any noise. Her whole body has sunk into the pillow. She is so deep in thought, she isn't even breathing.

"Besides, I'm going to die anyway. Everyone knows I'm going to die. As my father once said, 'Let me tell you something about death, Kantkiss.' *Dammit, my memory is terrible.*

"Anyway," I go on, "you could probably kill me now if you wanted to. You're probably plotting my murder right now."

Run remains completely motionless. It's a genius bit of acting. I don't know how she's doing it.

"As I was saying, I think forming an alliance would benefit us both. You can help keep me alive with your cleverness, and I can help you see over the tops of midsized rocks. I know you're shy and you want the other tributes to respect you as an independent baby, so I'll make things easier for you. I'm going to close my eyes and count to ten. If you don't want to form an alliance, then get away from me before I finish counting."

I don't hear a peep as I start the countdown.

"Ten . . . nine . . . eight . . . seven . . . uh . . . hm. . . . six! Just slowing down to give you the time you need and deserve. Five . . . one . . . now!"

I open my eyes to find Run right where I left her. Overjoyed by the formation of this new alliance, I lift Run from the goose down for a hug between allies. Run has turned a joyful shade of blue in celebration of our alliance. I'm a bit worried because she is having a violent coughing fit in my arms, but the cameras are loving this motherly moment.

R-i-i-i-p. Our snuggle is interrupted by a ferocious fart. Run may be tiny, but she sure produces a big smell.

"Whoa!" I shout, crinkling my nose.

Run laughs coyly, but the pungent odor emanating from her behind is no joke.

"Heh . . . eh . . ." I feel my throat starting to close. I throw my head back, hoping for clean air. Instead I am hit in the face with a stroller. From the sky, diapers, bags, bottles, and teddy bears are parachuting in. It's a baby shower! The sponsors love us. There's even a gas mask for me!

I bravely change Run's diaper. When the job is complete, I pop her into the stroller and head for fresher air. I find a perfect path beside the edge of a pond. Rays of light stream through the trees as I push Run along the water. For the first time since my LSBee experience, I feel at peace. I even wave to Gatsby Rockefeller's butler, who's pushing Gatsby up ahead in a luxurious adult stroller. It looks like a regal carriage.

"Halt! Stop this coach immediately!" Gatsby shouts from his seat. The butler obeys. Gatsby draws the curtains and emerges from the stroller's plush interior. He is pale and thin. He squints in the light. He wears a velvet jacket and flowing silken pants. It's standard attire for the lucky few residents of the old money district.

The butler presents Gatsby with a golden tray of jewel-encrusted swords. I stand back and draw my bow in defense. Then a strange thing happens. Gatsby falls to his knees in front of me.

"Don't kill me! Please don't kill me!" he yells, now hugging my legs and crying. His skin is even softer than Run's. While his arms hold me tight, his hands hang limply. He has lost motor function from never lifting a finger in his entire life.

In this moment I feel that Gatsby and I have made a connection. I don't know if I would call it a love connection, but on a scale from Carol to Pita, I'd rank Gatsby around Carol and a half.

"Allies?" I ask. I bet I could get some really awesome sponsor gifts out of this alliance.

"Yes, I suppose so. Can I . . . hold it?" he asks. I extend my hand. "No! What are you doing? Jesus Christ, get that filthy thing away from me!" he shouts in a fury. "I meant the baby. I would like to hold the baby. I have never touched one before. Back home, everyone has nannies for that sort of thing."

Sensing a prime opportunity for a bathroom break, I hand Run over to Gatsby. She's dazzled by his gold necklace. What a happy little alliance we make, the three of us!

When I return from the woods twenty minutes later, newspaper tucked under my arm, I find a crime scene. Gatsby's butler is artfully draping yellow caution tape from the surrounding trees. Run crawls toward him and tugs gently on his pant leg. Looking down at the baby, he screams and bolts into the woods.

In the center of the clearing is Gatsby's pale body, outlined in chalk. His face has turned an elegant shade of silver, befitting of his social status. Something has gone wrong. He is dead. I notice red marks around his neck. He has been choked, but how? We're all allies here!

Run crawls over to Gatsby. "Daaadaaadaaa," she whispers softly, grabbing the shiny gold chain around his neck and tugging it violently. Suddenly I understand. Run choked Gatsby to death.

"Run, you're right. I'm so sorry." She looks up at me with sad baby eyes. "I never asked you before forming that alliance with Gatsby, and that was wrong. I haven't been a very good ally today." She crawls over and sits on my foot. "No, Run— it's not okay. I should have listened to you. You had every right to kill Gatsby. You never agreed to be his ally. It was a very wise decision. Perhaps you saved both our lives today." Run bows her head. We share a brief moment of silence.

The hovercraft circles above us. When the door slides open, again I can hear two voices from inside.

"Can't this weekend. It's Jennifer's birthday."

"What are you two doing?"

"Made reservations at a bed-and-breakfast up on Lake Champlain."

"Nice."

"It'll be a working vacation for me. Trying to hire a maître d' is proving to be more work than I thought it would be."

"You know, my cousin is a maître d'. Maybe the two of you could—"

The conversation becomes inaudible as a mechanical ladder is dropped from the hovercraft. Several of the world's most beloved heirs and heiresses begin to descend one by one. The elites of District 6 have come to pay their respects to Gatsby. Stepping onto the dirt ground is the least dignified thing any of them has ever done. I watch as the likes of Goldman Sachs LXXXI, William Gates LV, and Paris Hilton XLV pay their final respects to Gatsby while jazz legend Duke Ellington LI performs sad trombone live. The last mourner is Jesus II, who says a nice prayer. The ceremony leaves me feeling unusually tender.

"You know, Run, I think we make a great team."

"Greauuuooo," says Run. I assume this is slang for "yes, of course" in District 11.

"Greauuuooo to you too, Run. What should we do now?"

Run sits up and begins shoving dirt into her mouth. "Diiiirrrrr," she says, which is District 11 slang for "Varsity pack."

"No . . . really? Do you think we could?" Run tumbles forward. She is playing dead. "You are truly a fierce competitor, Run. This is a very ambitious plan."

Run has just suggested that we kill the Varsity pack. It's a bold move. Suddenly, I wish Pita were here. I am craving a snack. I'd even accept whole-wheat bread at this point. But could I break bread with the enemy? Anyway, I have to listen to the rest of Run's plan.

Run is shoving more dirt into her mouth. "Good idea," I say. "The way to weaken the Varsities is by targeting their food supply. But how can I get to it? It must be heavily guarded."

Run looks up at me. Our eyes lock. "Eyes," I say. "You want me to use my eyes. Brilliant! I will survey the area for booby traps. You can keep a lookout here."

Run starts to cry. "Yes, I understand, we definitely need a signal. How about this: If you're ever in danger, take these baby wipes and climb up this tree. When you're at the top of the tree, sew all the wipes to make a flag. Remember, I need to be able to see this flag from several miles away. As long as the flag is green-and-white-striped, I will know you are safe. If I see a yellow-and-red-checkered flag, I'll know you're in trouble."

Run giggles and lets out an earth-shaking fart. This is my cue to leave. I head toward the center of the arena, where the Varsities are stationed with their massive food supply.

When I reach Camp Varsity, I hide behind a heavily padded field goal post and survey the area. It's the size of a football field and looks just like one. Plastic cups are littered about midfield, left over from Archie's birthday kegger. He and the others are running hundred-yard sprints. I look over toward the food stash: it's piled high with delicious rations. It sits in front of a large white house with a patio. Above the front door, hung crookedly, are the Greek letters ΠΚΑ.

I gasp. Someone is already going after the food supply. Dogface! Surely the food must be heavily protected, yet she hops and skips right toward it in plain sight. Dogface makes it to the food pile unscathed. The Varsities are too engaged in their games to notice. She grabs a single stick of gum from underneath a bunch of bread, cookies, and water, then me-anders into the woods.

I'm thinking through my plan, when Broadway show tunes begin to drown out the Varsities' chill John Mayer playlist. The theater district tributes must be near. I hear them singing a song to the tune of "Gee, Officer Krupke" from *West Side Story*:

> *Deeeeeeear kindly land of Peaceland, you gotta*
>   *understand*
> *These games work when you plan 'em, but now they're*
>   *out of hand.*
> *Archie's got a football, none of us have food.*
> *Goodness gracious, everybody's screwed.*
> *Dear good land of Peaceland, we're down on our*
>   *knees*
> *Because of neurotoxin from those damn LSBees*
> *Our vision is hazy, our mouths taste like tin.*
> *Gee, good land of Peaceland—you win!*

The song distracts the Varsities from their afternoon workout. Archie grabs his steel football and beckons the others to follow. They set out with murder on their minds.

With Camp Varsity vacant, the coast is clear for me to make my move. I sprint the length of a field, pausing only for a small victory dance when I enter the end zone.

BWOMMP BWOMMP. BWOMMP BWOMMP. I count two sad trombones in the distance, signaling the death of the theater district tributes. I flash a smile at the nearest camera and say, "There won't be any encore for *them* tonight." Then, pleased with myself, I also say, "That show's run is over." Before moving on, I add geniusly, "District Ten just took its final bow." And finally, "The only place they'll see another standing ovation *is at their funerals.*"

Satisfied, I move on with my plan to destroy the Varsities' food. I must take tiny bites of all this delicious food to ruin it before they return. I bite everything—raw steaks, live chickens, pieces of pie. Once I start biting, I just can't stop!

When I've bitten everything, I stick a couple of Twinkies in my pocket for Run and hide behind a tree. She won't care that they're bitten. She shouldn't be eating whole Twinkies at her age anyway.

I'm so full. I think I'll just rest. I think I'll just go into a food coma right here behind this tree. Yeah, that'll be nice. The back of this tree is the perfect place for a food coma. I puke up a few bites before passing out.

10 ◎ ▶

I awake to the sounds of the Varsity tributes groaning. Kantkiss 1, Varsities 0, for now at least. I step out from behind the tree into a puddle of my own vomit. I feel well camouflaged here. I peer down into Camp Varsity, where Archie blows a whistle, calling a time-out. I start jogging over to join the huddle, but then I remember, *Kantkiss, that's not your team!*

Archie is shaking with rage. The whole huddle is jiggling because of it. Luckily he is yelling, because otherwise I wouldn't be able to hear him from this far away. It sucks how many important plot developments you can miss just because you aren't standing close enough.

"Defense! What happened out there?" Archie shouts.

"We dropped the ball, bro."

"Don't mess with me. You know and I know that this is bigger than high school football, bigger even than college football. This is the big league. This is Peaceland's top-rated *The Hunger Games*! What happened?"

"Well, when we went into the woods to kill those drama geeks, another kid, one undeserving of the title 'tribute,' took small bites of everything except the butter sticks. The butter sticks were eaten in their entirety."

A female voice shrieks that can only be coming from Mandy. "Ew! I am definitely not eating some nerd's leftovers," she says, flipping her hair into Archie's face and hiking up her denim miniskirt.

"You never eat anyway!" responds another Varsity.

"Thanks!" says Mandy.

"Silence!" bellows Archie, pulling a slightly nibbled megaphone from the food pile. "There will be no more bites today! We can't risk any injuries. The food pile must be destroyed."

"Right on, Archie! Let's do an explosion!" another tribute shouts. "But first, let's take a break and get some snacks from our other perfectly intact food pile."

I gasp. Other perfectly intact food pile! I look to my left. There it is, another food pile, peeking out coyly from behind a boulder at the other end of Camp Varsity.

"What? Who put that there? Our nutritionist did not authorize a second food pile! I repeat: that is an unauthorized food pile. It too must be destroyed," proclaims Archie.

Archie pulls a bunch of dynamite from his pocket and sets it up around the food piles, wiring everything just right for a mind-blowing simultaneous explosion. He is so dangerous!

BOOM!

I cry as the food pile I just ate from turns into ash and

flame. All that remains is this half-eaten Twinkie I saved for Run. I stuff it into my mouth, savoring every last morsel. Run doesn't have to know about this.

The food pile is reduced to a smoldering crater. From what I can tell, Archie is about to lose it.

"I'm going to kill the scum that did this!" Archie exclaims.

"Weren't you going to kill him anyway?" one of the other Varsities asks.

"Yes, but now I am going to kill him in a very *special* way!" Archie yells back.

He explodes with anger and punches a tree with his bare hands. He rips some hair out of his head just prove that he isn't bald. He puts on a baseball cap with the rim pointing backward to cover up the bald spot he has just created. Will there be no end to his rage?

Archie calms down. He pulls on some boxing gloves and continues punching the tree just for exercise.

"You know what?" he says, throwing a jab at the tree. "It's an honor to be here. We were chosen out of hundreds of thousands of children. There was no way to know that we were the ones who were going to get picked, which is why we fought our way toward the stage to volunteer, killing several civilians in the process." Jab, jab, hook. "It's good to be here, killing children. I enjoy that. I enjoy slaughtering children. It's awesome to be on TV when you're killing people!"

Archie puts on a great performance for the cameras. There are tears in my eyes. I wish I could stick around for the rest of it, but I'm getting pretty nervous about the special way Archie's going to kill me. I decide it's best to clear the area. I retreat into the woods with a death wish upon me. I need to find Run before it's too late! I remember the signal we agreed on. Green-and-white-striped flag, Run is safe. Red-and-yellow-checkered flag, Run is dead. I scan the tree canopy for flags, but there are none in sight. What could it mean?

I head back to the spot where I left Run. Except for a few diapers piled in an obvious attempt to build a tepee, the site is abandoned. I decide to follow a nearby stream. Maybe Run climbed into a basket and floated away to avoid becoming the victim of a cruel and oppressive regime, like that clever baby Moses in that book.

I take some berries from the trees and throw them into the stream for good luck. One time some girls made fun of me for being so superstitious. Well, look where I am now! I'm in the Hunger Games.

I haven't found Run, and I'm getting worried. Not just about her but about myself also. Even though I am the main character of this story, there is no way that I will win the Hunger Games. I, the narrator, have told this entire book and there's still like fifty pages left. So I'll probably die in the next few pages, and someone like Run will take over the storytelling or something.

I find one of Run's fires. It's just a bunch of spit, because Run is a baby. She must be close! I feel like her mother, even though we've only known each other for a few hours. I know

I spent most of those hours eating, but I was eating for two. As a mom, I have to tell myself that Run is still alive. There's no possible way she could be dead, not in a game where the object is to kill everyone—including babies.

I follow Run's trail of spit back to where I left her. The trail takes a sharp left into some shrubbery about five feet away. There she is! She's lying helplessly at the foot of a shrub, and I am suddenly filled with motherly pride. Run must have taken her first steps to get there!

There is little time for celebration, though. Run is about to die.

I hadn't noticed the tribute from the tanning cream district because his deep tan blends seamlessly with the tree trunk behind him, but I am suddenly alerted to his presence by the huge pitchfork he is now preparing to plunge into Run.

I pull out my bow and prepare to defend my ally. "Don't shoot!" the tanning cream tribute screams, like a wuss.

"I'm not going to shoot you," I say, stalling. "Let's be friends." The tribute looks at me, smiling. While I keep him distracted, Run grabs at his shoelaces, tangling them into a complicated knot. Then I smell something. Run has just deployed the biggest fart of her life.

The tribute gasps for air. He staggers forward but is tripped by his shoelaces. I shoot him midfall, just to put him out of his misery. *BWOMMP BWOMMP.*

"We did it!" I yell to Run.

Then I realize I've made a very insensitive comment.

Run is pinned to the ground, skewered by the fallen tribute's pitchfork.

"Oh Run, don't die! Not like this!"

There is no reason to BS Run at this point. She knows that she is about to die. It's my job to make sure she dies with honor.

"This will only hurt a little," I say, pulling the pitchfork clean of her flesh with one violent tug.

One thing I think Run will appreciate is flowers. I go and pick a bunch of beautiful dandelions that are next to a tree.

"Gagaga," she says. I love listening to her *gaga* and *gala* mouth noises. I wish that humans spoke that way all the time. Run starts crying as I sprinkle the remaining flowers in her eyes.

"I know," I say, "I don't want to say good-bye either." I choke as I start to remember all the great times we had together. Yesterday, for instance, was one of the best days of my life. I start to sing Run a lullaby.

As I walk through the valley of the shadow of death,
I take a look at my life and realize there's not much
    left,
'Cause I've been blastin' and laughin' so long that
Even my mama thinks that my mind is gone.

My final words to Run are "Run, die." She dies in my arms. Well, not really. She dies in the grass, and then I pick her up so that I can say that she died in my arms. Don't get me wrong, I would do anything to get her back. But you have to admit, it is kind of cool to say that someone died in your arms.

The saddest trombone yet sounds from above. *BWOMMP BWOMMP.* I move away from Run's body so the hovercraft can collect her before another tribute comes along and ruins my beautiful flower art. I find a hiding place not too far off where I can watch Run embark on her final journey. The hovercraft floats down from the sky. When its main door slides open, I hear two voices coming from inside.

"I agree with you, one hundred percent."

"Thank you. I just wish Jennifer would see it that way."

"She will. Keep in mind, you're sinking your whole life savings into this restaurant. She's bound to be a little nervous."

"She says she's worried about the money, but that doesn't stop her from coming home from the mall with a new pair of shoes every week."

"Look, just explain to her that when it's all said and done, you're the one who—"

The doors seal shut, and the hovercraft grabs hold of Run's body and begins sucking it heavenward. Her body floats up, hits a tree, and falls back down. It looks like she is going to make it on the second attempt, but they drop her from even higher. She bounces off several branches on the way down, before getting snagged on a low-lying holly bush. Eventually, the hovercraft operators sweep Run's body to the side and bury it under some leaves. Run's time in the Hunger

Games has finally come to an end. I am proud that my ally went down fighting.

I know at this moment that every single camera in Peaceland is focused on me. I smooth my hair and very stealthily unpick my wedgie.

I look up to see a tiny silver parachute bringing a gift just for me. Unlike Run's body, it manages to steer clear of the trees. I tear away all the wrapping paper and open the box. The first thing I see is a card that reads "From District 11." *How nice*, I think. When I peel back more wrapping paper, I find the gift: a ticking bomb! I have no idea how to use a bomb, but it's the thought that counts. The kind people of District 11 sent me this bomb to thank me for being such a great ally to Run. Obviously they were hoping I'd be able to use it to kill other tributes. There is nobody else around, so I toss it into a nearby pond, where it explodes, killing thousands of fish.

All of a sudden, a voice comes bellowing from the sky. It's Greg the Announcer. "Eh peepo cannaw winna Ooga Gehs!" he shouts.

His supervisor then comes on the mic. "Eight people can now win the Hunger Games," he clarifies.

I count in my head. Since Run just died, there are now eight people left in the Games. *Me, Archie, Mandy, Smash, Dogface, the girl from District 8, the boy from District 9, and Pita.* That means that all of us will live! Yay!

"Just kidding!" the supervising announcer says, cracking up. "Not all of you can win. However, we have decided that *two* tributes can win the Hunger Games. Resume killing one another!"

I immediately think of Pita. I sniff the air for the scent of bread. Hm . . . the direction of the wind tells me I must proceed westward. Within a few minutes I come upon a trail of bread crumbs. I begin to follow them, certain they'll lead to Pita.

My mind is consumed with one thought: *How does Pita have the resources to make such amazing bread in the arena?* I follow the delicious little morsels, popping each one into my mouth to confirm that yes, this is the same marble rye that has been blowing my mind all afternoon. This goes on for hours, and despite the occasional misidentified rock throwing me off his track and causing severe damage to my molars, I soon sense his sweet doughy scent growing stronger.

Suddenly, I hear a whimper coming from a clearing on my right. I peer around a tree and take in a depressing scene. It's the female tribute from the red light district, crying softly as she uses the trunk of a young tree as a stripper pole. Dozens of parachutes are raining down around her, each containing a dollar bill. "I can't use these here," she weeps, giving a sad little shimmy and tucking a bill into her bra strap out of habit. "Just send me food or a weapon. Money is not helping me here." I have to admit I feel bad for her and in a way admire her spirit. "You go, girl," I mutter under my breath, as I pull an arrow from my quiver and release. I never thought I would be the kind of person that would kill a stripper, but this just feels right.

Right before the sad trombone sounds, I hear a loud crack behind me and turn around to see Smash glaring at me from behind a stump where a tree stood a moment ago. He pushes over several other trees and pounds his fist against his chest. He rips open his shirt and roars, pushing me to the ground and standing over me as if he's about to body-slam me to death.

"You die now," says Smash.

"You *will* die now," I correct him, but this only makes him angrier. Smash jumps up in preparation for the fatal body slam, but then stops.

"You friends Run?"

"Some of them run. A lot do other forms of cardio," I reply. This guy is wasting my time.

"No!" Smash explodes. Then he takes a notebook out of his pocket and consults it. "You friends . . . *with* . . . Run?" he asks.

"Yes," I say.

"You try life save?" Smash asks.

"Yes, but I prefer Tic Tacs."

"No! You try save . . . Run . . . life?"

I nod.

Smash thinks hard for a minute, then steps away from

me. "Just this one time. Smash let you go. Because of Run. Now you and Smash even. Understand?" I nod vigorously.

"Cut!" A camera crew emerges from the woods, the director leading the way. "Cut. Smash, babe, unreal. Totally scary but totally tender. The thing is, Martin was getting some b-roll of birds in flight, so we're going to need you to do that again. You good, man? You want some lemonade? We're going to have someone touch up Kantkiss's makeup and then we'll try this again in five."

After six takes, a photo shoot, Smash changing his mind, a near-death experience, Smash changing his mind again, and another take, I am free to go. I take off running toward Pita's mouthwatering smell. Along the way I carefully gather every crumb in my mouth. There are children starving in postapocalyptic Africa, after all.

Before long the bread trail ends in a small clearing, and the delectable smell of dough reaches its climax. I know he must be nearby, but a quick survey of the area shows no sign of Pita—tree, tree, rock, cave rock, ten-tiered wedding cake with an ornate floral design, stream, tree. Frustrated, I sit on a rock and try to think what might have happened to him. Could he have climbed a tree? He doesn't exactly have the center of gravity for that, but in a totally masculine and desirable kind of way. Sure, he doesn't have Carol's height or athleticism, but that can be gross sometimes. I take another desperate look around the area when the most peculiar thing happens: the wedding cake blinks.

"Pita! You're right here in this clearing disguised in your

signature baked goods camouflage!" I scream at the top of my lungs. Someone could have heard me, but if I limit my ability to express myself, then am I really even *me* anymore?

The cake smiles, and Pita rearranges his body fat back into normal boy form. "I'm so happy you found me. Did you follow the trail?"

"It was the highlight of my day! That hint of cinnamon in the bread is really something special. You have a gift."

"Thank you, Kantkiss, that means the world to me. But that's not bread." He blushes. "That's my dandruff."

"Huh. Well, come on, let's go kill enough teenagers to win this game." I begin to walk away but sense that Pita isn't following me.

"Kantkiss, I'm hurt. It's my finger. I don't think I can move." I look over to him now and to my horror see that his finger is covered in blood. "Oh sorry, that's frosting. I was experimenting with natural dyes. There are these flowers that make the most gorgeous crimson hues." He licks the frosting off to show me the damage on his finger.

"What happened? Is it broken? Infected? Jammed?" I ask. I can't see a thing.

"No, I think . . ." A single tear rolls down his cheek. "I think it's still tender from when I cut it the other day fighting Archie. But we're going to fight this thing." He puts his hand on my shoulder and wipes his eyes. "Together we can get through anything."

"Is that it? Stop being a little girl and walk it off."

He doesn't seem to hear me. "I know, you're right, it is

really brave of me to offer to help with the hunting and the gathering and the killing of others, but with my injury that would be foolish." He raises his head in a dignified yet pained manner. "I'll just let myself heal in that cave over there and you can take care of all that stuff."

"Fine, we can make camp there for the night. Let's go."

I walk toward the cave but soon hear a polite little *ahem*. I turn around and see Pita looking at me expectantly, glancing down at his finger and sticking out his lower lip. "Ouchie, ouch!"

"Yes, dear." I sigh as I gather Pita into my arms and roll him to the mouth of the cave. Just when I begin to relax in the knowledge that no one can find us here, a tree collapses beside me and Smash jumps in front of Pita, roaring.

"Now two die!" he declares.

"Hello," says Pita, extending his hand, "How have the Games been treating you?"

Ignoring Pita's good-natured small talk, Smash grabs the trunk of the tree he pushed over and prepares to club us to death with it.

"Excuse me," pipes up Pita, "your shoelace is untied."

Smash looks down and sees that Pita is right. "Smash could have tripped," he reflects. After a moment he puts down the tree trunk and backs away from us. "Just this one time. Smash let you go. Because of shoelace. Now you and Smash even, understand?"

Pita begins to protest that it was his pleasure to point out that Smash's shoelace was untied and that there is really no need to repay him, but I put my hand over his mouth until Smash walks away.

Once Smash is gone, I turn to Pita. He just saved my life. "Hey," I say sweetly, "remember when you wanted to go to the kissing station during training and I rejected you? Well, if you want to practice here, I'd be down."

Just when the words leave my mouth, a shower of silver parachutes fills the clearing outside the cave. Buttitch has sent us champagne, oysters, chocolate-covered strawberries, candles (unscented), candles (rustic cedar), a string quartet, a heart-shaped Jacuzzi, and a television playing the clip from *The Lady and the Tramp* where they eat spaghetti and kiss.

Suddenly the string quartet stops playing. The cellist leans over to me and says, "Excuse me, Kantkiss? The name's Friedrich, huge fan. Anyway, Buttitch said that this might happen and asked me to give you this message: Kiss Pita."

What? I think. I have never kissed a boy before. Kissing has never even entered my mind. But if Buttitch, a disgusting old pervert who clearly doesn't have my best interests at heart, wants me to do something sexual on live television, I figure I better do as he says.

I approach Pita. I put one hand on Pita's shoulder and give it a squeeze, raising my eyebrows high and then bringing them down low to demonstrate my interest. He places his hand on my cheek and looks deep into my eyes, stroking my skin tenderly. I swat him away because we really don't have time for his crap. Since I've never kissed anybody before, I'm not entirely sure how to proceed. One thing I do know is that a good kiss involves a lot of tongue—like a *ton* of tongue, everywhere. Going straight for the mouth feels a little forward, so I decide to start with the cheek and drag my tongue slowly up his face and across his forehead, then back down his nose. I nibble a little because he smells really good and then lick his lips with confidence. Confidence is very important.

"Open sesame," I order, "the captain is ready for landing." With that I pry his mouth open with my hands and stick in as much of my face as I can manage. His delicious smell overwhelms me. This is heaven. The cellist rubs his hands together in agreement.

After another sixty seconds of this, I extract myself and take two steps back. To my delight, a dozen more parachutes fall to the ground with gifts ranging from a lame water purifier to an awesome puppy dressed in a sailor outfit.

Suddenly I understand. The sponsors like it when I kiss things. I tilt my head up to the sky and address them directly. "How about some of this"—I rub my tongue along the floor of the cave—"and this"—I lick up every last ant off a boulder—"and a little bit of this!" I shyly approach a nearby tree and give it a tender peck in the intimate spot where a branch merges with the trunk. The sponsors must have run out of money because I get nothing for these efforts. When I turn back to Pita, he seems to be reenergized.

"I'm starting to feel better, like my old athletic self. See, I used to be a ribbon dancer." He laughs. As he sways his hips to an old routine, I can't help but be reminded of the time Carol was not a ribbon dancer but instead single-handedly

supported his family with his incredible hunting skills. He's
out there somewhere, his abdominal muscles rippling in the
sunset's glow, glistening with sweat after a hard day's work.
And here's Pita, slipping on a bit of leftover frosting and rolling away in the cave's slight incline. *I burn with desire, but for
whom?*

I get the grim feeling that this impossible choice will
plague me for the rest of my life and that nothing—even the
political future of all Peaceland—will overshadow its impor-
tance.

Pita announces that he's hurt himself again, and after
thirty minutes of crying in my lap, he's tuckered himself out
enough to go to bed. We decide to share my sleeping bag for
the body warmth but agree that kissing is far too exhausting
to do more than once a day. We settle in, and before long the
Peaceland emblem blazes in the sky, followed by a picture of
Run. As the smooth jazz comes on, I feel a warm trickle on
my leg.

"Pita, what is that?" I ask.

"What?" Pita replies.

"Did you just wet the bed?"

Pita clears his throat, "Uh . . . no, it's apple juice. From a
sponsor. Don't drink it."

Relieved, I fall asleep.

The next morning Pita insists that he's still in pain, so
I have to spend all day hunting to put food in our mouths.
When I return a few hours later, exhausted and sore, I am ap-
palled by what I find: the champagne bottles are empty, the

strawberries are gone, and the sailor puppy is dead. Meanwhile Pita is lounging in the Jacuzzi and listening to the iPod that *I* earned yesterday with my awesome kiss.

"Well, that took a long time," he says. "Were you planning on spending *any* time with me today?"

"I was getting you food. What happened to Sailor Puppy and why hasn't he been given a proper burial?"

"So I'm your slave now? Because I can't hunt, I have to do everything for you?"

"You know, you're being real sassy today, Pita. Remind me again, who's providing for us? That's right, this gal." I point to myself. "I work hard all day, so I expect to come home to a crackling fire and a nice foot massage and *no dead puppies* stinking up the place. Is that so much to ask?"

Before Pita can respond, Greg the Announcer's nearly incomprehensible voice is projected throughout the arena. After he repeats himself four times, I can understand the gist of what he says: "Remember, two tributes can both win, so if you're arguing in a cave right now like Pita and Kantkiss, you should probably stop fighting and start being a little more in love."

I sigh, understanding the subtle implication that the audience wants another kiss. I stick my tongue out as far as it will go, but then Greg the Announcer's supervisor speaks, "One more thing: you're all cordially invited to a Buffet at the Cornucrapia where you'll each be given what you need the most. Come and get it!"

"Kantkiss, do you know what this means? They could

have a Band-Aid for me, maybe even aspirin!" Before I can respond, Pita exclaims, "You're right, though. It's too dangerous for me. Thanks so much. It would be great if you could go get it."

"I'm sorry, you can't take ten minutes out of your busy schedule to get rid of the dog, but you expect me to go and risk my life for an injury you're probably faking anyway? This is not the delicious boy that I fell in love with."

Pita sniffs and turns away from me in shame. "Do you even find me beautiful anymore?" he asks.

"I don't know if I ever did." With that, I gently scoop up the puppy and walk outside looking for a good burial site. Just as I'm realizing how difficult it will be to dig a hole with my bare hands, a parachute drops down containing a metal shovel. *Great, another brainteaser from Buttitch. What could it mean?*

I put the shovel aside and try to think about what Buttitch wants me to do as I scoop up dirt for the puppy's grave, but I can't concentrate with Pita wailing in my ear. "Oh no, Kantkiss, you are not coming back into my cave when you're covered in dirt like that." He puts a hand on his hip and shakes a finger at me. "You're going to mess everything up, and guess who's going to clean it up tomorrow? Just because I don't hunt doesn't mean I don't work."

That's when I understand the meaning of the shovel, and with a quick smack on the back of the head, Pita is out like a light.

◀◎12

I spend the next few hours rolling Pita out of the cave and into the exposed wilderness. Some fresh air would do him good while I'm at the Buffet.

I build a fire next to Pita's unconscious body to keep him warm, and tell the quartet to play as loud as they can throughout the night, so that Pita will be entertained when he comes to. I am about to leave for the Buffet when I remember that the audience wants to see more of the star-crossed lovers angle. I draw my face in close to Pita's and exclaim, "I'm pregnant!" Then I leave.

It takes me almost five hours to get to the Cornucrapia because I have a long conversation with Bob, a friendly cameraman, and get sidetracked. When I finally reach the Buffet, I am famished, and I'm disappointed to learn that they haven't even started serving appetizers yet. Like me, the other tributes will all be hiding in the woods that surround the Cornucrapia impatiently making do with breadsticks and glasses of water. I think of who is still left in the games besides Pita and me: Archie Nemesis, his girlfriend Mandy, Smash, Dogface, and the boy tribute from District 9. Even though the District 9 tribute doesn't have a memorable name or any recognizable characteristics, I remind myself that he has as good of a chance of winning the Hunger Games as anybody.

Suddenly the ground splits open and a large, white table emerges from inside the horn of the Cornucrapia. Seven backpacks are on the table, each of which has a number between one and twelve written on it. *Those mysterious numbers could mean anything.* "I'm number one!" I exclaim, instinctively rushing toward that backpack.

Before I can snatch it, I take a moment to honor my contractual obligations to the Hunger Games.

"Darn!" I exclaim, looking straight at the camera and scowling. "It doesn't look like any of these backpacks contain *Professor Moura's Cinnamon-O's.* That is what I need more than anything else this morning! *Professor Moura's Cinnamon-O's*: end the Hunger Games inside your stomach."

Even before I finish plugging my breakfast cereal, I see a figure darting out of the Cornucrapia. It is the tribute from District 9. He has been hiding in the Cornucrapia all night, right under our noses. As he grabs one of the backpacks and starts to run away, I gasp. What a stupid strategy! Every idiot knows you don't go first in a situation like this! Archie Nemesis pops out of the bushes and kills him immediately. *BWOMMP BWOMMP.*

I breathe a sigh of relief (my sixteenth of the Games). I'll never have to pretend to know that tribute's name again. Each time I ran into him, I would awkwardly call him "man" or "dude," and I think he was beginning to catch on.

Thankful for the distraction, I make a run for the table. I only get a few yards before a knife hits me straight in the forehead. It doesn't hurt much, because the handle side hits me rather than the sharp side, but it is enough to make me draw my bow in anger. Another knife whizzes past my head. As I load my bow, I see that my assailant is Mandy, and she's about to throw a third knife. I fire an arrow at her. It completely misses Mandy, but it does hit a squirrel straight through the eye. *Celebrate the little things, Kantkiss*, I remind myself to keep from getting frustrated. *You might still be in mortal danger, but that was some damn fine squirrel hunting there.* Right when I am beginning to feel better about myself, another one of Mandy's knives hits me in the forehead. This time it's the sharp side. I fall to the ground.

"Well, well, well . . . If it isn't my old friend Kantkiss Neverclean," Mandy gloats as she approaches me. "Not so clever with a knife sticking out of your forehead, are you?"

"Oh my God!" I tremble as I pee myself. "Please don't kill me!"

Mandy opens her jacket to reveal an impressive assortment of knives. A fixed blade knife, a gut hook knife, and a few menacing butter knives. She selects a particularly nasty-looking one with a long, curved blade and holds it up to my face.

"Consider this knife," she begins. "Consider its handle, in particular. Does anything about this handle strike you as odd, Kantkiss? That's right. It is made out of wood. Look around us, Kantkiss. We are surrounded by *trees.*"

I panic. "Pita is hiding by the cave next to the triangular rock by the stream!" I interrupt. "Kill him instead of me!"

But Mandy continues as if she didn't hear me. "Webster's dictionary defines victory as an act of defeating an enemy or opponent in a battle, game, or other competition. But to me, victory is as much a process as it is an act. I'd like to take a few moments to explain why I think that is."

I feel woozy. I remember some advice my mother gave me when she was a healer. "Avoid getting knifed in the forehead," she would say. I struggle to remain conscious before deciding it's not worth the effort.

When I come to, Mandy is still delivering her lengthy victory monologue. "But enough about my childhood. It's in the past now. And, if you think about it, isn't time the true enemy?"

I am about to go back to sleep when Mandy leers over me. "But *your* time is just about up, Kantkiss Neverclean."

She raises the knife over her head and gradually brings it down toward my neck as she counts down from forty. "Thirty-nine . . . thirty-eight . . . thirty-seven . . . thirty-*six* . . ."

I make my peace with the world. I pray that Prin grows up to be a beautiful woman and that Mother gets evicted from our house. I think of Carol, with his incredible shoulder muscles and jet-black hair, and Pita, with his man boobs and politeness, and regret that I will never get the chance to choose between them. I sadly reflect that I never got to know the *real* Slimey Sue.

"Four . . . three . . . two . . ." Just as Mandy is about to say "one," an excited voice cuts her off.

"Pretty girl! Pretty girl!" Smash runs straight at Mandy, arms outstretched and a huge smile on his face. You have to hand it to him. For a guy with an IQ in the low forties, Smash has an impeccable sense of dramatic timing.

"Pretty girl! Pretty girl! Pretty girl! Pretty girl!" Before Mandy can stop him, Smash grabs her in his arms and starts petting her head. "Pretty girl . . . ," he coos.

"Put me down!" Mandy says indignantly, but before long she stops struggling. *Oh my God, he's crushing her!* Even with her eyes rolled into the back of her head and her tongue sticking out, I have to admit she still looks pretty hot.

"Pretty girl?" Smash asks hesitantly, shaking Mandy's body. "Pretty girl!"

BWOMMP BWOMMP. The sad trombone confirms his worst fears. "You loved too hard, Smash," I tell him.

"Why love hurt!" Smash bellows, as he sets Mandy's body on the ground. Then he picks up a rock and turns on me. "Now you hurt!"

I say my final prayers, just like I learned in Sunday school: "Our Bernette, who art in heaven, hallowed be thy name . . ."

Smash is about to hit me with the rock, but then he stops, his mind elsewhere. "In cafeteria . . . during training sessions. Aunt Kantkiss invite me to sit at table."

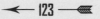

I remember the incident Smash is taking about. Pita and I had asked him to join us at lunch.

"Just this one time, Smash let you go." Smash says. "Because of lunch. Now you and Smash even. Understand?"

I nod fervently. I run to the table and grab the two District 12 backpacks. As I hurry back toward the safety of the woods surrounding the Cornucrapia, I hear Archie Nemesis arriving at the table after me. He looks inside his backpack and pumps his fist in the air. "Yes! Gatorade! Electrolytes!" he exclaims. But then he turns to Mandy's body.

"You do this to my girl, bro?" he asks, walking over to Smash and shoving him.

"Maybe." Smash considers. "Smash no remember."

"Not cool, dude," Archie says. He takes his metal football and throws it at Smash as hard as he can. It's a perfect spiral that hits straight in the chest, but Smash keeps standing like nothing hit him. "Sick!" Archie mouths.

Smash picks up Archie and lifts him above his head. He is about to break him in half when he pauses. "In tribute parade stable. Quarter fell out of Smash pocket. Archie could have take quarter and bought gum ball, but Archie gave quarter back to Smash."

Smash sits down for a second, thinking hard as he cradles Archie in his arms. Finally he speaks. "Just this one time, Smash let you go. Because of quarter. Now you and Smash even. Understand?"

"Sure, bro," Archie says, catching his breath. "We're cool."

As Smash walks away, Archie throws a spear in his back. I can just make out Smash's last words before he collapses on the ground: "He who overcomes by force hath overcome but half his foe!"

BWOMMP BWOMMP. I have bigger things to worry about than mourning Smash. One of the backpacks I am carrying is very heavy and there is still a huge knife sticking out of my forehead. I am bleeding profusely. *No matter,* I tell myself. *If I make it out of the Hunger Games, I'll be so rich I can pay somebody to have a regular forehead for me.*

As I walk through the woods, I hear a sound coming from nearby the Cornucrapia. I turn around to see Dogface wandering aimlessly into the open. She doesn't seem to realize that the Buffet is going on around her. After a little while she stumbles on the table with the backpacks and peers inside the only remaining one. Delightedly, she pulls out a ball of yarn and starts to play with it.

Ignoring for some reason another perfect opportunity to kill Dogface, I head back toward Pita. The backpacks are really starting to weigh me down. I sit down beside a nearby boulder and open Pita's backpack. It contains a Sweet Dreams sleep mask and a pair of earplugs, which confuses me until I remember a comment Pita made yesterday. "The thing I could use most in the world right now is a nice, long nap," he said, yawning as he read his newspaper. I struggle to contain my anger as I think about how I nearly died twice for this backpack. I am almost angry enough to fall in love with Carol instead of Pita, but then I remember that whiny tone of voice Pita uses when I don't give him enough attention, and I am back to not knowing which one to choose.

My own backpack is much heavier than Pita's, and I have

no idea what it contains. It keeps making strange, yelping noises, particularly when I drop it on the boulder. It almost sounds like it's saying, "Please stop dropping me."

I am about to thank my sponsors for this awesome noise-making backpack when a pair of hands emerge and unzip the backpack. Eventually a tall, handsome man in his mid-forties crawls out of the backpack.

"Hello, Kantkiss," he says, brushing himself off. "I am your father figure."

"What?"

"I've been hired to be a strong paternal presence for you. To give you love and support," he says.

My bottom lip begins to quiver.

"My poor little girl," he says, giving me a hug. "Without a father figure in your life, you have turned into a moody brat!"

"I'm sorry I poked you with sharp sticks when I thought you were a noisemaking backpack, Father Figure," I say, hugging him back. There are tears in my eyes.

"No, *I'm* sorry, Kantkiss," my father figure says. "I'm sorry for being absent for so many years. I'm sorry I missed all your yelling recitals and dogfighting games in that terrible high school you go to in the Crack. I'm sorry that I didn't get to see you turn into the strong, beautiful young woman standing before me." Now both of us are crying.

"Come on," my father figure says after a while, "Let's get that knife out of your forehead."

After we yank the knife out, my father figure takes me fishing in a nearby lake, where we have a nice, long daughter-

and-father-figure chat. "I want to hear everything, Kantkiss," he says. "Catch me up."

I tell him my life story. "Are you sure you're not thinking of *Battle Royale*?" he interrupts me.

"No, the teenage angst makes it different," I say.

"Of course it does," my father figure reassures me. Father figures understand everything. "It sounds like you have had a very difficult life. Tell me, how did you avoid killing people when you were chosen for the Hunger Games?"

"Sorry?" I ask.

"When you were forced to compete in the Hunger Games, how did you avoid committing murder like the Capital wanted you to? You know, how did you maintain your sense of morality in a difficult situation?"

I gulp. "Actually . . . uh . . . I've sort of . . . er . . . just been killing people without thinking about stuff like that."

My father figure drops his fishing pole in the lake. "What?"

"Yeah," I say, "I've . . . uh. . . . kind of just been trying to win the Hunger Games."

"Didn't you consider right or wrong at all?" my father figure asks, horrified.

"I did a little bit before the Hunger Games started," I say, "but once I got to the arena, I sort of just stopped thinking about it completely."

"So you . . . you've killed a human being?" my father figure asks.

I tug on my collar nervously. "Yup. But if you really think about it, it's really like self-defen—"

"Kantkiss," my father figure manages after a long time. "By killing other confused teenagers, you are committing a very evil act. Plus you are on *live television*. If you refused to kill other tributes, you would not only remain a good person, you would also send a powerful statement that could bring down one of the most evil regimes in history."

"But if I do anything rebellious, the Capital will hurt my family!" I argue.

"It is completely understandable to think of your family in a situation like this," my father figure says, "but you have to consider the scale of what we are talking about. The Capital enslaves *millions* of people, forcing them to live in horrific conditions. This is a regime so evil that they genetically engineer *bees* to attack the *children* they force to fight to the death *every year* for their *entertainment*. If you get a chance to take down this regime, you have to take it and keep your personal matters in perspective. I love you, but bringing down this terrible regime clearly takes priority over any one person's individual welfare. Anybody with a basic sense of community can see that. Plus, even if you don't want to make a dramatic, rebellious statement, it is very easy not to kill people. Just don't do it. Don't commit *murder*, Kantkiss."

My father figure's words make a lot of sense. Maybe rebelling against an oppressive political regime should take priority over my teenage love triangle with Pita and Carol. Maybe I should think twice about murdering a fellow teenager, even when this incredibly evil regime tells me I shouldn't.

I am so grateful for my father figure and his wisdom. If I spend enough time with him, I feel positive that I can return to being a sensible, emotionally well-adjusted young woman capable of dealing rationally with her difficult situation.

"All right, I'd better be going," he says abruptly. "I was only hired for the afternoon."

"Father Figure!" I cry out, as he climbs back into his backpack.

"I love you, Kantkiss." He kisses me on the forehead as he zips the backpack up. "Please don't murder anybody else."

Then, as quickly as he entered my life, my father figure leaves it forever. I tearfully walk back toward Pita and the cave. On my way, I see a baby deer pick a flower with its mouth, which cheers me up immediately.

When I get back to the cave, I don't see Pita anywhere. Everything else is how I left it. The fire is still burning. The quartet is still playing next to a large apple tart. The entrance to the cave is still well exposed, to let fresh air in. I bite into the giant apple tart as I think the scene over.

"Ouch!" exclaims the apple tart. Pita has done it again.

13 ◎ ▶

Pita waits with bated breath while I recollect the grim details of what happened at the Buffet. "There were backpacks, and Smash was there," I say.

"Hm," says Pita.

"Oh, and he's dead now," I remember.

"Weird."

There is an awkward lull in the conversation. I am happy to let it die. But Pita adores small talk. "So, where is Smash from?" he asks, genuinely interested.

I lean in and kiss him, this time because I want to. It feels good, and I instinctively reach for one of his breasts and start to massage it tenderly. Pita pops his left foot as he moans softly, moving his round, doughy head to invite me to kiss his neck. Just then a parachute floats to earth outside the cave. The distraction brings us out of the moment, and Pita jumps away from me, covering his breasts in indignation. I step out of the cave and retrieve Buttitch's latest gift. It is a box full of circular, foil-wrapped candies. I unwrap the foil and find it's not candy in there at all: the box is full of balloons. Slippery balloons. I'm not sure why Buttitch would send us these slippery balloons in this time of great hunger, but I inflate all of them and decorate the cave like it's my birthday. After the nightly announcements, I fall asleep to the sound of smooth jazz.

At dawn, I smell Pita's early morning farts and open my eyes. Through the cracks in the rocks of the cave, I see the smoky gray of an overcast day. I hear the pitter-pat of a light drizzle. The Rainmakers must have caused this weather to torture our minds by depriving us of sunlight, trying to give us seasonal affective disorder. There is no other possible explanation.

"Will the Rainmakers ever let us be?" I ask Pita.

He looks at me and starts to blink uncontrollably. Back home, when we need to talk with each other but are worried about being overheard by Pacemakers, we blink at each other to communicate. Blinking slowly and normally means everything is fine, and blinking rapidly is a way of expressing something controversial, like *The Capital sucks!* or *Slimey Sue for president!* Perhaps Pita is trying to tell me something that he doesn't want anyone else to pick up on. "Is there something you want to tell me?" I ask him. "Do you have more jokes about Pedro the cameraman's huge mole?"

"No," Pita whispers to me. "I wanted to tell you that I get scared when I'm not near you. I want to go hunting with you today."

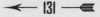

As Pita tugs gently on my shirt, worried that I am not giving him enough attention, I can't help but remember how Carol never does this but instead has hunted wild boars ever since he was six years old. *But does Carol know how many cups of sugar you need to make a cinnamon roll?* I think to myself.

"Okay, Pita," I say, resisting my urge to kiss him passionately, "you can come hunting with me today."

"Yes!" Pita jumps in the air, and his big doughy head collides with the roof of the cramped cave. "Kantkiss and Pita, hunting together forever!"

We pack what little supplies we have left. We say goodbye to the quartet and set off from the cave, heading toward the Cornucrapia. I move stealthily, making sure to avoid stepping on any crunchy leaves. Pita's walking strategy ruins my attempt to be inconspicuous, though. He insists on wearing light-up sneakers, which he pounds into the ground extra hard to ensure full illumination with each step.

"Shut up!" I hiss at him, "You're scaring off the animals!" But he doesn't hear me because he has burst out singing:

District Twelve is the Telemarketing District.
It's the District above Eleven and below the now-
*   defunct District Thirteen.*
It's responsible for the calls your house receives at
*   dinnertime,*
And boy, do we have a mighty good time!

Would you like to order the deluxe package?
It comes with a seal of authenticity.
No, you cannot speak to my manager right now,
He is currently speaking to somebody else!

He sings this again and again. I realize that if I'm going to catch any animals today, I will have to separate myself from Pita and convince him that he's doing something worthwhile.

"Oh, Pita?" I ask him gingerly.

"*Would you like to order the deluuuuxe—*yes, darling?"

"Could you collect some big rocks for a fire pit?"

I see Pita's grin fade from his face as he begins to tremble. "But . . . won't that mean not being with you?"

"Here," I say, "I'll give you a piece of my shirt. You can hold it tight when you begin to feel afraid, and it will be just like I'm there."

I cut off a piece of my sleeve and give it to Pita, who hugs it and smiles. He waves a temporary good-bye and hustles off into the forest in search of big rocks.

I begin setting rabbit traps, stepping on slow squirrels, and looking for birds that have fallen out of trees. Everything is much easier without Pita around.

BWOMMP BWOMMP. I'm startled to hear the sad trombone. Who could have died? Oh no! Could it be Run? Sweet little Run? Wait—she's already dead. *Phew.* Then I remember that it could also be Pita! He was still alive! I hurry in the direction Pita went as fast as my legs will carry me.

I get to a clearing and see Pita lying motionless on the ground.

I shake Pita's body and slap him a few times. No response. My whole body goes numb with shock. Why on earth did I let this idiot out of my sight? I don't see any visible wounds on his body. He must have had a heart attack. "You ate too many carbs!" I say between slaps.

"Huh . . . what?" Pita says groggily after a moment, drooling as he opens his eyes and squints in that confused, irresistible way of his.

"Pita! You're alive!" I exclaim, slapping him some more because he had me so worried. "*Never* do that again!"

"I was just napping." Pita stifles a yawn. "It was a long walk between when I left you and this clearing, and my legs got so tired."

I try my best not to blush, because every time Pita talks about his legs, I get excited. "But if you're not dead, then who did the sad trombone sound for?" I ask.

"All I know is that I collected some mighty fine rocks before I went to sleep," Pita says. "I really did you proud, baby. Look."

I look in the direction Pita is pointing and gasp. Lying next to a small pile of rocks is Dogface. Her eyes are rolled into the back of her head, and there is gravel all around her mouth. Her cold hand grips a large rock with a bite taken out of it.

"I promise there were more, Kantkiss," Pita says in a whining tone of voice. "It's just not fair!"

I am about to take Pita in my arms and kiss him like there's no tomorrow, but just then the hovercraft descends to pick up Dogface's body. The doors slide open.

"That sounds like a perfect location."

"It is. We'll have to renovate the kitchen. But other than that, it's ready."

"I can't wait to go. There's no good seafood place in the Capital right now."

"Ours will be the best. Top-notch stuff."

"And the financing is all taken care of?"

"Well, that's what I wanted to talk to you about. How would you feel about coming in as a part owner?"

"Jesus, Dave, I'm not sure if—"

The hovercraft doors slam shut. As it flies away, an icy breeze fills the air. I shiver slightly. "Are you cold?" I ask Pita.

He shrugs. "I'm actually a little bit warm. I would give you my sweater, but then I might get cold."

Rainmakers. They have created this breeze. There is no other plausible explanation for it. If we get cold enough, then we will have to fight to the death, just to keep warm. Those monsters. *Where can we go to warm up?* I remember that there is a café inside the Cornucrapia that serves hot chocolate and has central heating. That is where they are forcing us to congregate.

"To the Cornucrapia!" I exclaim.

"Fine," says Pita. "But did you hunt any food?" He rubs his belly. "I haven't had a snack in nearly an hour."

Bashfully, I realize that I didn't catch any birds in my

bird trap—a pane of glass suspended between two tree trunks. And I don't want to disturb the birds in my birdhouse. "Uh . . . sure," I say, slyly picking some bright orange berries from a bush behind my back. "Lots of food."

"Kantkiss!" Pita exclaims when I show him the berries. "Those are poison berries. My father used to bake with them, and it led to so many lawsuits. If you eat one of those things, you will die in a matter of minutes!"

"Oh," I say, about to toss them on the ground. Pita stops me, though.

"Keep them just in case," he says. "Who knows how hungry I will get later?"

As we walk toward the Cornucrapia, the clouds shift through the satin sky, and pretty soon the sun is beginning to drop, creating purple and orange things I never learned how to describe with science. The rapidly approaching season finale of the *Hunger Games* has me excited. I look into the camera and say my catchphrase, which I imagine is emblazoned on hundreds of thousands of T-shirts and lunch boxes throughout Peaceland by this point. "It's Kantkiss time!"

By the time we reach the Cornucrapia, the breeze has died down. Classic Rainmakers: starting and stopping the breeze at seemingly random times to disorient us and make us turn against each other in confusion. Still, it is too warm for hot chocolate now, so Pita and I wait outside the café. After half an hour, I hear a rustling from the edge of the forest and see Archie Nemesis running straight for us.

"*Eeeeeeek!*" screams Pita, sexily hiding behind me.

But today Archie isn't the confident, angry sociopath I've grown accustomed to. His eyes are puffy and red, and mucus is pouring from his nose. He's followed closely by what look like several very small, ugly panthers. But these aren't bloodthirsty, ugly panthers at all . . .

"*Trannies!*" Pita and I scream in unison. Archie barrels past us and tries to scale the horn of the Cornucrapia, followed closely by Pita, but I stand my ground. One of the trannies jumps on me and licks my hand lovingly. I look closer. They're puppies! And they are so soft and cuddly. They gather around me and I give them hugs and then tickle their bellies while they lick dirt off my face. I look up to Pita, wondering why he isn't playing with even a single puppy.

"Those trannies are . . . fr—freaks!" He gesticulates wildly.

I look at the puppies more closely as they happily play with one another. One of the puppies is much bigger than the others. He pins his friend to the ground and is about to lick his face, but then pauses thoughtfully and lets him go. Another of the puppies—a purebred Staffordshire terrier— has a polite bird that always follows him around and deferentially collects bones for him. Another puppy keeps walking into a tree. I gasp when she finally turns around: Dogface! Her facial features are exactly the same as before, only now they look normal because she has the body of a puppy. These puppies are the fallen tributes!

Whatever the Rainmakers did to those dead tributes, it is delightful. I squeal with joy when I see the tiniest puppy of all, Run, who bumps into me with eyes that haven't opened yet and then falls over adorably. I scoop her up and put her in my pocket, where she licks my hand from time to time. If I win the Games, I'll keep her as my purse dog.

Suddenly a steel football whizzes past my head, missing by only a few inches. I turn and see Archie Nemesis panting by the base of the Cornucrapia. His eyes are still puffy and red, and it is clear that dog allergies have reduced him to a shell of the all-district athlete who started the Hunger Games. *The old Archie would have knocked my head straight off*, I think nostalgically.

The puppies excitedly follow the football and roll it back to Archie with their little wet noses, eager to play fetch, as Archie frantically tries to fend them off. His face is swollen beyond recognition and he is getting weaker by the second. I walk over to him because I want to play with the puppies some more.

"Kantkith . . . Kantkith, don't kill me like thith . . . ," he begs.

In all the puppy excitement, I had completely forgotten about killing Archie, but I'm glad he's reminded me because I definitely want to. I look over at Pita, who is so terrified by the puppies that he is crying. *If I kill Archie now, I can kiss this stud all I like.*

"Thorry, Archie," I say, adopting his strange manner of speaking, "I have to get out of thith arena."

"Pleath don't do thith, Kantkith!" he cries. I cover as many of the puppies' eyes as I can while I draw my bow.

"Pleath! Pleath!" he pleads. "I love you, Kantkith!"

I lower my weapon. "What?"

"I have . . . uh . . . alwayth loved you, Kantkith!" he declares. "You are the prettieth girl I've ever theen!"

"Do you really mean that, Archie?" I ask, my voice tender and vulnerable.

"Yeth! Yeth, I do!" he exclaims excitedly.

"What are you waiting for?" Pita asks between cowardly sniffles. "Kill Archie! I want to get back to my bakery!"

I hesitate. Pita keeps shouting, "He is clearly lying to you to save his own life, Kantkiss! Archie is a complete psycho and he just tried to kill you two minutes ago! You've got a good thing going here." He points at his tear-filled face. "Stick with it!"

"I'm thorry, Kantkith. I never meant to hit you with that football," Archie explains. "I wath aiming at the tree behind you, and I feel like an idiot becauth I nearly hit you inthtead."

"That's okay, Archie," I say. I can't believe it. *Archie Nemesis is in love with me!* And as I suddenly realize, I am in love with him too. I have been since the first time I saw him glare menacingly at me at the Opening Ceremony. He has always been the perfect man for me, I just didn't realize it. I wish Mandy were still alive so she could be jealous of me.

"Come here, you old lug." I swoop in and kiss Archie. It is hard to get to his mouth because his cheeks are so swollen, but I have had plenty of practice moving aside Pita's cheek flaps.

"Oh, Archie!" I swoon. "You're *wonderful*."

"Get thothe dogth off of me!" He pushes me away with all the strength he can muster. "Uh . . . Pleathe do that for me, thweetheart?"

"Sure thing, baby." I walk a few steps away from Archie. "Come here, puppies!" I beckon, clapping. "*Good* dogs!"

While Archie gasps for air and starts to recover, I play with the puppies, but I am distracted by Pita's loud sobs.

"Suck it up, dough boy," I tell him. "Archie is the complete package."

"I'm just worried he will hurt your feelings," Pita says, his voice wobbling. "And my feelings are hurt because I miss all the attention you gave me. I . . . I'm so hungry and I just want to go *home*." He breaks into another fit of sobs, but I resist the urge to throw myself into his arms. I'm Archie's girl now.

But Pita's homesickness brings up a good point. Only two of us can make it out of here alive. There can only be two champions. If I don't kill one of these heartthrobs, the Hunger Games will go on forever. *Unless* . . .

"Quick, Pita!" I say. "Give me those poison berries!"

He hands them to me and, one by one, I throw them at a nearby camera as hard as I can. "Take that! And . . . *that*!" I figure it's only a matter of time before the Rainmakers will concede defeat. "And a little bit of *this*!"

I throw nearly all the poison berries with no result. The Rainmakers are playing hardball. As I pause to reconsider my strategy, I see that Archie, my true love, is standing up again.

"Hello, sweet thing," I greet him. "Feeling better?"

He staggers toward me. When he is a few steps away, I lean in to kiss him. He takes out a plank of wood and lifts it above his head, but then drops it and brings his hand to his face to sneeze.

"Is there a dog nearby?" he manages.

"Oh, sorry!" I exclaim, taking Run the puppy from my pocket and placing her on the ground a few steps away from Archie. "What were you doing with that wooden plank, darling?"

"I, uh . . . wanted to give you a prethent, baby. Didn't you mention thomthing about liking wooden plankth?"

"Oh, Archie," I say, kissing him on the forehead as I admire how solidly constructed the wooden plank is, "I love it!" I have the most thoughtful boyfriend ever. But I am suddenly jolted out of my romantic reverie when I look over at Pita.

"Stop it!" I shout desperately. Pita is picking up one of the poison berries and is about to put it in his mouth. "Don't kill yourself because I chose Archie over you!"

"Huh?" Pita says. "Oh, it's not that. I'm just so *hungry*."

"That's too bad, Pita," I say. "I don't care how hungry you are, you can't eat that—" I stop speaking. I have just had another brilliant idea. If Pita eats the berry and dies, then I can live in the woods forever with Archie and raise a family with him. The Rainmakers will make life hard for us by creating fires and tornados and things, sure. And there won't be much for the kids to do when they grow up, but at least this way I will be able to stare into Archie's harsh, unmerciful eyes to my heart's content. "Er . . . never mind," I finish my sentence.

Pita returns to his poison berry. He is just about to pop it in his mouth when he sneezes, blowing the berry into a puddle. This is the last straw. Pita sits down and cries softly. After a moment he picks up the berry from the puddle and prepares to eat it, but now I can't let that happen. I can't explain it, but seeing him sitting there, covered in snot, I feel a renewed sense of passion for Pita. I might be Archie's girlfriend now, but I can't just sit back and let such a sexy man die.

"Wait!" I say. I have just had another brilliant idea. "Gather round, guys," I tell Archie and Pita. "You know how the Capital values the lives of the tributes so highly?" They both nod. "Well, if we threaten to kill ourselves by eating the poison berries, then they'll do anything to save our lives. Sound like a plan?"

"Does it ever!" exclaims Pita excitedly.

"Let's do it!" chimes in Archie.

"On the count of three, then," I say, handing them both poison berries. I look directly in the camera and address the Capital. "Unless you want your gladiatorial event to end with the only three remaining tributes dying painful, climactic, awesome deaths, you'd better do what we say—" I am cut short by the beeping of a car's horn.

BEEP! BEEP! We look up to see a red convertible speeding through the clearing. In it are three tributes: two from District 4 and one from District 8. *Huh. I guess not all the other tributes are dead after all.* "We're going to win the Hunger Games!" the driver from District 4 boasts, but he is so distracted that he drives off a cliff. The car explodes in a burst of flames, leaving no survivors.

As the sad trombone sounds three times, Archie, Pita, and I return to our plan. "Are you ready?" I ask. They nod.

I take a deep breath and start counting. "Three post-Mississippi . . . two post-Mississippi . . . one post-Mississippi . . ."

Right when I am about to reach zero post-Mississippi, the loudspeaker crackles to life and Greg the Announcer frantically shouts, "Herzledewoog! Wahhammihmih! Nowooleybog!"

Greg's supervisor intervenes. "All right! All three of you can win! Just don't swallow the berries!" I throw my berry on the ground and pump my fist in celebration as Greg's supervisor continues speaking, obviously thinking that his microphone is turned off. "Greg, I'm sorry. You know that nobody is a bigger supporter of our Jobs for Felons program than I am, but this just isn't working out. Please clear your desk."

"Mazzydagor!" Greg curses angrily, before the loudspeaker finally cuts out.

Whatever, I think. *I just won the Hunger Games!* "Yippeee!" I exclaim, turning to Pita to celebrate. But Pita is sprawled out on the ground, bright orange juice dripping down his face.

"Pita!" I shout. "Pita, why are you ignoring me? Pita, you're being a dick!"

"I was . . . so hungry," he gasps, before closing his eyes and going silent.

A million different thoughts race through my head at once. I barely notice the loudspeaker as it blares on for the final time: "Ladies and Gentlemen, the victors of the Seventy-Fourth Hunger Games: Kantkiss Neverclean and Archie Nemesis!"

Applause plays live over the speakers, followed by a slow clap, which doesn't catch on. When I hear Archie Nemesis speak, it seems like he is a million miles away.

"Woo hoo!" he's saying. "I'd like to thank my mom and dad for pushing me to become a Varsity tribute since I was a little boy. I couldn't ask for better parents! I'd like to thank my trainer, Adolf Evilman, for all his guidance in the arena. They said that a team of stock villains couldn't win the Hunger Games, but we showed them, buddy! And of course, I couldn't have done it without the big man upstairs." He folds his hands in prayer. "Lord Bernette, our president and divine creator."

I am leaning over Pita's sensual, convulsing body. The sad trombone hasn't sounded yet. There is still hope. A part of me wishes I had visited the antidote station when I was at the Training Center. But I ignore my regrets and resolve to push forward, just like I learned at the proactive attitude station.

An ambulance hovercraft lands on the ground and a team of doctors puts Pita on a stretcher and rushes him away.

"*Wait!*" I yell, grabbing the hovercraft and trying to hold on as it takes off for the hospital. "Treat *my* injuries first!"

I only sulk for a moment before two more ambulance hovercrafts land. "Do you want to ride in my hovercraft, Archie?" I ask suggestively.

"Nope," he says, grabbing a pretty nurse by the waist—I think she is his cousin—and leading her into the ambulance. I have never been this in love with anyone.

As I walk past the severed arm of some unlucky tribute, I am reminded of home. Even amid the death and decay of the Crack, there is beauty. For every rotting carcass, there are two poppies. This thought consoles me as I pick up Run the puppy and Archie's amazing wooden plank. Then I get in the last hovercraft, ready to return to the Capital.

• • •

Gradually, I wake up from a deep sleep I don't remember falling into. Everything is hazy. I dimly hear a voice—I think it belongs to Effu—saying, "Don't resuscitate! Stop feedin' dat girl intravenously!" I am in a white hospital room surrounded by nurses, doctors, and—sure enough—Effu Poorpeople. This part of the Hunger Games is never televised, and I feel privileged to get an exclusive, behind-the-scenes look.

Everybody falls silent when they see I have opened my

eyes. "She's awake, mon," Effu says after a moment. "It's so good to see ya, darlin'!"

I brush aside her pleasantries. Only one thing is on my mind. "Archie!" I exclaim. "Has he texted me?"

"I'm sorry, dear," replies Effu. "Perhaps his cell phone is outta batteries?"

"That must be it," I say, thinking fondly of Archie. *What a good guy.* "How about Pita?" I inquire absentmindedly, my mind still fixated on that awesome wooden plank Archie gave me. "Did he survive?"

"The last time I checked, it was touch and go," Effu says. "I've been busy overseeing ya medical care da past few hours."

"Well," I say, rising, "I should go say hi to people. I haven't seen Circle in ages."

"Naturally," says Effu. "By da way, are ya goin' to Colonel Srivatsa's soiree tonight? He's a horrid little weasel of a mon of course. Still, one feels obliged . . ."

I am taken aback. Aside from that do-not-resuscitate thing, Effu is being incredibly nice to me now that I have won the Hunger Games. It's almost like . . . *I'm rich!* Holy crap! I am so rich! I can buy all the squirrel meat I want now! The thought fills me with joy and I excitedly jump out of bed.

"I can't tonight," I say, quickly adjusting to my new socio-economic role. "I have a date with a large mouse steak. I'm going to eat it *all* myself. And afterward I am going to sleep on a bed . . . with *blankets*!"

Effu scoffs. "New money . . ."

As I leave the room, I feel weird. There is something weighing me down, making it difficult for me to walk upright. I gasp when I see my reflection in a mirror: my boobs are gigantic!

"Oh yes," Effu begins to explain, "Buttitch and I tried to stop da doctors from doing dat when dey healed you, but—"

I stop her midsentence. "I *love* them, Effu." Not many seventeen-year-olds in the Crack can compete with these bazookas. What an awesome day. I walk down the hallway to see if Pita is still alive and find Buttitch in the first room I enter.

"Buttitch!" I greet him warmly. "How's it hanging?"

"Uh . . . good, good!" he says, hurriedly draping a sheet over his desk. "Congratulations on winning the Games."

"What do you have under that sheet there, buddy?" I ask.

"Just some boring old paperwork," he says. "Listen, I need to talk to you about something very important."

"Go ahead," I say, pulling up a chair next to Buttitch's desk of bulky paperwork.

"Would you like some coffee?" Buttitch asks me.

"Don't mind if I do," I say. He hands me a cup and I take a big, long sip.

"This may come as a surprise to you," Buttitch begins. I sip even more coffee. "But when you threatened the Capital on live television and made them change the rules to their own game, they weren't too pleased."

Psssshh. I spit out all my coffee. "Wha?"

"President Bernette is watching you very closely," Buttitch continues, "and if he thinks that you are a threat, he will have you executed."

"But . . . but . . . President Bernette is a merciful and benevolent ruler! Everybody knows that!" I protest, sitting up in disbelief. I still haven't adjusted to the weight of my modified chest, and I flop forward onto the desk, pulling the sheet off in the process. "Buttitch!" I declare when I look up. "This isn't paperwork."

Buttitch's desk is full of strange items of all shapes and sizes. There are several vials of medicine, a wide assortment of weapons, some camouflage gear, and every type of food and drink you could imagine. Next to one pistol I spot a note saying "Make sure she gets this before sunset," from Mark Zuckerberg XXIX.

A rough-looking man wearing a leather jacket walks into the room. "I'll give you fifty bucks for the stolen camouflage suit," he announces. "And that's my final offer." Buttitch frantically shoos him away and then turns to me.

"Oh right. Sorry, by paperwork I meant birthday present. This is all a birthday present for my, uh, mother," Buttitch says, hastily putting the sheet back on.

"Buttitch," I say, taken aback. "That is *very* thoughtful of you!"

"Yeah, anyway," he continues, "I've got a plan to keep you alive. Just renounce your title and declare Dogface the official winner of the Hunger Games. That way all the heat will be on her, and she can take that heat because she's dead."

"But how will that change what I did with the berries?" I ask.

Buttitch doesn't seem to hear me. "She was a sure thing!" he explodes. "Seven-to-three odds looked like easy money! And then she had to go and eat those damned rocks!" He pounds the desk with his fist, then composes himself. "Trust me, Kantkiss," he says after a while, "declaring Dogface the winner of the Hunger Games will solve all our problems."

"I'll think about it," I promise. "By the way, do you know what happened to Pita?"

Buttitch lowers his head solemnly. "He didn't make it."

I fight back tears. "But surely with their technology, the Capital could have found an antidote for the poison!"

"Oh, yeah," Buttitch says, "the doctors treated that easily. No, the trouble came when they gave Pita cosmetic breast reduction surgery. There were complications and he died on the operating table. It was too bad, I had two hundred bucks on him surviving."

I rush out of the room, furious at the whole world. Why would a kind, loving Bernette let such a sexy man die? Does Bernette even exist? *Of course he does*, I reason, brushing aside my atheistic doubts, *I saw him give a speech a few weeks ago*. Still, I haven't been this sad since my dad died, or at least since my father figure returned to his backpack. I wonder if I will ever experience happiness again, like that time I won the Hunger Games. *That was sick.*

I run back into my room and collapse on my bed, crying harder than I have cried in years. I just wanted to live the District 12ian dream: hunt squirrels, avoid getting executed, repeat. How did things get so messed up? I always thought I might kill teenagers, but I wanted it to be on my terms. I never wanted to be a pawn in the Capital's stupid game. And now Pita's dead! If he had stayed in District 12, he could have lived another ten, maybe fifteen years. I cry and cry and cry.

I look up and notice a figure sitting in a chair in the corner of the room. She must have been here the whole time.

"Dry ya tears, girl," the figure says in the strange, affected accent of the Capital. "Ya learning about da big woman tings now." It's Effu.

The last thing I expect from Effu is a sympathetic ear, but she walks over to my bed and strokes my hair tenderly. Effu is really nice to rich people.

"Dis world is nutten but trouble," she reflects. "Ya gotta obey da politicians or else ya get trown in da prison. Ya gotta look after da younguns and put 'em in da Hunger Games, but you know dey gonna get blown to bits. Dat poor boy with da jiggly man bits, Pita, I thought he was gonna make it. I shoulda known betta. All dese tings add up and make ya real sad sometimes." She pauses for a second but then perks up. "But when ya feel dat way, ya just gotta rememba: don't worry about a ting, 'cuz every little ting's gonna be all right."

She stays by my bed for a while, stroking my hair, and I start to feel better. Then a nurse carries Run the puppy into my room. Somebody gave her a puppy sweater that is way too big for her, and it slips off as she chases her little tail around. I start feeling downright awesome.

"Dat's a real cute puppy," Effu says.

I play with Run the puppy until Cinnabon enters my room and pushes everybody else out. He is here to dress me for my post-Games interview with Jaesar Lenoman, which is my big chance to prove to everybody that I am on the Capital's side. I can't wait!

"Where's your team?" I ask. It is unusual to be dressed by Cinnabon before meeting with Flabbiest and Venereal first.

"In jail, thank God!" he says. "Kantkiss, I am so sorry about how they 'prepped' you. If I had any idea, I would never have hired them. It makes me sick to the stomach!"

"Huh," I say. "So what dress do you have for me this time?"

"Say what?" Cinnabon asks, his expression blank for a moment. Then he explodes in frustration. "Oh *dammit!*"

"What's the matter?" I ask.

"Nothing, nothing," he says. "I'm, uh . . . still upset about what happened to Pita, that's all. Close your eyes and I'll go get your dress."

I do as he says. I hear somebody leave my room and close the door. Then, after a very long time, the door opens again and footsteps hurriedly enter my room. I hear somebody shout, "Hey! That belongs to the optometry department!" from the hallway, before the door is slammed shut and locked.

"There," Cinnabon says at last. "You can look now."

I open my eyes, but something is different. I have a narrow range of vision on my left side, and my depth perception is way off. When I look in the mirror, I see I am wearing an eye patch. No. Way. *Cinnabon has transformed me into a lady pirate!*

"Oh, Cinnabon," I gasp, "you've outdone yourself!" Ghosts and warrior mummies are scary, but a lady pirate is something else. A lady pirate is . . . is . . . adventurous, and cunning, and . . . *"Beautiful!"* I mouth, my eyes still glued to the mirror.

"Yeah, uh, since you have, uh, steered the ship of . . . er, the Hunger Games, now you are a, uh, pirate," Cinnabon orates. This blows my mind. *Cinnabon is a genius.*

"Aye, aye," I agree. Now I am ready for anything the Capital throws at me.

It is time for the post-Games interview. A hovercraft takes me to the studio, and I mentally prepare myself for what is to come: Jaesar Lenoman jokes. I can hear him warming up the audience from backstage. "So get this. I was watching the end of the Hunger Games, and a telemarketer called. He just wanted to celebrate!" I grit my teeth, wishing I had died in the Hunger Games.

My name is finally called, and I walk onstage. Archie Nemesis emerges from the other curtain. *I love that dude!* "Let's get out of here," I say to him, but he keeps walking to the love seat next to Jaesar Lenoman, and I join him, cuddling up close. He gets up and sits in another chair.

After a few more torturous jokes, Jaesar introduces this year's highlight reel. Given the amount of footage from which to choose, it's up to whoever puts the reel together to determine what tale to tell. One year, the footage told the story of a small group of freedom fighters who roam the far reaches of the galaxy in hopes of destroying an evil empire, and another year the film took the form of a homage to silent cinema, with all the tributes replaced by title cards.

This year the highlight reel has an upbeat tone, much like a circus picture. As the opening credits fade out, the sound of a piano and tenor saxophone fill the room. "Yakety Sax." What a beautiful theme to watch my competitors die to.

With the song playing, footage of Pita, Archie, and the others getting attacked by the LSBees comes on the screen. *Pita*, I muse as he appears on the screen, swatting away a particularly nasty-looking bug. *Will he make it out alive? I hope so.* Soon after, the camera finds a girl Varsity tribute who slips on honey. The noise of a whoopee cushion accompanies her error. The audience laughs, and I can't help laughing myself. That girl was a bitch.

After the LSBees incident, more blooper footage occupies the screen. A boy from District 2 pees himself as Smash approaches with a blood-rusted hammer. A girl from District 6 slips out of a tree and onto a remote mine. It's a good time.

Then Jaesar Lenoman begins the interview. "As we all know, every year the Hunger Games can be won by finding a flag hidden somewhere around the Cornucrapia, resulting in the release of all tributes. But you two have survived this year's competition by finding a flag hidden in each other. Kantkiss, when did you know Archie was the one?"

"Huh?" I ask. "You don't want to talk about the rebellion?"

Jaesar pulls on his collar, gesturing for me to shut up. "Let's just focus on you and Archie." He laughs nervously.

But I know the truth, and I think, *Jaesar, how naïve you are. Rebellion is all we'll be talking about. Love is revolution, a kind of coup d'état and cultural reprogramming in its own little way.*

"I realized Archie was my soul mate the moment he gave me that wooden plank," I say, taking it out of my purse to show the audience. "Isn't it beautiful?"

"True romance," Jaesar says. "And you, Archie?"

"Ditto," Archie says, texting on his cell phone. He doesn't seem in love with me, but I guess everyone has a different way of expressing feelings.

"Brilliant. And about that little berry incident . . . ," Jaesar says gingerly.

This is it. This is when I sink or swim. I speak slowly. "I wanted to know what those berries tasted like."

Archie nods his head in agreement. "We all did."

"Great!" Jaesar says. I look over at President Bernette in the audience, who gives me a big thumbs-up. I breathe a sigh of relief. I have overcome the obstacle of the final interview. I endure a few minutes of horrible pirate jokes before Jaesar signs off to the viewers across Peaceland and I go backstage with Archie. *Finally, some time alone with Mr. Perfect.*

"I don't love you, Kantkiss," he says, when I try to kiss him.

"Because you can't love me?" I ask. "Because you're afraid that if you love me too much, it might hurt you? Because it hurts to be in love, which is what you actually are?"

"Nah."

With that, he walks away. I wonder if I'll ever see him again. Perhaps in the sequel to this book, *The Adventures of Kantkiss and Archie*, but one can never be sure.

Back in my room, I consider what Archie told me backstage. His words didn't suggest that he loved me, but he must love me. "I have a really good feeling about this relationship," I tell Run the puppy.

As I pack my bow and squirrel bodies into my suitcase, I consider how far I've come since Super Fun Day. Back then I hadn't even kissed a boy, let alone killed one! I made so many friends during the Hunger Games, friends that remembered me until the day they died. *The Hunger Games were the best days of my life.*

"Hurry up, mon," Effu calls from the hallway. "Ya train is here."

I wonder what the future will hold. Maybe I will stay in District 12 and refuse to help the rebellion because I am so obsessed with boys. Maybe I will move to Canada or some other normal democracy. Either way, I'm rich. *Yay!* There is only one thing making me sad: the Boy with the Head. I miss Pita.

I hear my door creak open. "I'm coming, Effu," I say. "Chill out."

But Effu isn't standing in the door. At first I think nobody is there, but then I hear the sound. *Woof! Woof!* Standing on the floor is a very chubby puppy wearing a bagel around his neck. He sheepishly totters over to me and whines impatiently until I put Run the puppy in my purse and give him affection instead. As I scratch the puppy's head, I notice it is completely round and smells like cinnamon.

"Pita!" I hug him. "Let's get back to District Twelve."

ABOUT THE *HARVARD LAMPOON*

The first volume of the *Harvard Lampoon* appeared in February 1876. Written by seven undergraduates and modeled on *Punch*, the British humor magazine, the debut issue took the Harvard campus by storm. United States president Ulysses S. Grant was advised not to read the magazine, as he would be too much "in stitches" to run the government.

The *Harvard Lampoon* is also the proud author of the classic parodies *Bored of the Rings* and *Nightlight*. Contrary to popular belief, the *Lampoon* is not responsible for any of Stieg Larsson's work.